MUSIC EXPRESS

YEAR 7

BOOK 4 MUSICAL STRUCTURES

Series devised by
Maureen Hanke

Book 4 compiled by
Maureen Hanke
with Elizabeth Bray
and John Stephens

A&C BLACK • LONDON

BOOK CONTENTS

AUDIO CD TRACK LIST

TRACK	CONTENT	TRACK	CONTENT
1	*A fifth of Beethoven* by Walter Murphy (from the film *Saturday Night Fever*)	14	*Mind swap* – kick drum theme
		15	*Mind swap* – ping-pong theme
2	*A fifth of Beethoven* (A section)	16	*Mind swap* – open hatch theme
3	*A fifth of Beethoven* (B section)	17	*Mind swap* – ping-pong with reverb theme
4	*Ideas bank A – melodic theme 1*	18	*Mind swap* – crunchy bass theme
5	*Ideas bank A – melodic theme 2*	19	Extract from *Un granito de arena* by Ibrahim Ferrer
6	*Ideas bank A – melodic theme 3*		
7	*Ideas bank A – melodic theme 4*	20	*Ideas bank B – rhythmic theme 1*
8	*Overture* by Killa Kela	21	*Ideas bank B – rhythmic theme 2*
9	*Ideas bank A – rhythmic theme 1*	22	*Ideas bank B – rhythmic theme 3*
10	*Ideas bank A – rhythmic theme 2*	23	*Ideas bank B – rhythmic theme 4*
11	*Ideas bank A – rhythmic theme 3*	24	Extract from *Quadrille* (ABA)
12	*Ideas bank A – rhythmic theme 4*	25	Extract from *Quadrille* (ABACA)
13	Extract from *Mind swap* by Rob Bullough	26	*Montagues and Capulets* by Rob Bullough

CD-ROM CONTENTS

PRESENTATION

Unit overview

Learning intentions lessons 1–6

PRINTOUTS

1 Unit overview
2 Learning intentions lessons 1–6
3 Musical contrasts
4 Musical contrasts – keyboard
5 Notation revision
6 Composing melodic themes
7 Ternary form – background information
8 A typical midi sequencer
9 Ideas bank A
10 Ideas bank A – keyboard
11 Beatboxing
12 Composing an A section using a midi sequencer
13 Mind swap – listening sheet
14 Composition notepad
15 Composition notepad – keyboard
16 Keyboard effects
17 Key words
18 Ideas bank B
19 Ideas bank B – keyboard
20 Rapping
21 Composing a B section using a midi sequencer
22 Assessment criteria
23 Finishing touches
24 Finishing touches – keyboard
25 Finishing touches – ICT
26 Rondo form – background information
27 Quadrille
27t Quadrille – teacher's answer sheet
28 Montagues and Capulets
28t Montagues and Capulets – teacher's answer sheet
29 End of unit evaluation sheet

VIDEO CLIPS

1 Beatboxing – kick drum sounds
2 Beatboxing – snare drum sounds
3 Beatboxing – hi-hat sounds
4 Ideas bank A (beatboxed)
5 Ideas bank B (beatboxed)
6 Beatboxing skills showcase – performed by TyTe.

MIDI FILES

ternary.mid

ideas.mid

quadrille.mid

TEACHER INFORMATION

Sample lesson plan

Using ICT

Using electronic keyboards

Using a midi sequencer

Using this CD-ROM

First published 2006
by A&C Black Publishers Ltd
38 Soho Square, London W1D 3HB
© 2006 A&C Black Publishers Ltd
ISBN 10: 0-7136-7365-6   ISBN 13: 978-0-7136-7365-4

Teaching text © 2006 Maureen Hanke, Elizabeth Bray and John Stephens
CD/CD-ROM compilation ©℗ 2006 A&C Black
Edited by Rebecca Taylor and Harriet Lowe
Inside design by James Watson, Susan McIntyre, Jocelyn Lucas and
Carla Moss. Cover design by Jocelyn Lucas
CD-ROM interface design by Tatiana Demidova
Cover illustration © 2005 Graham Hutchings
Inside illustrations © 2006 Kanako Damerum and Yuzuru Takasaki
Audio CD sound engineering by Stephen Chadwick at 3D Music Ltd
Video clips filmed and edited by Jamie Acton-Bond at Miloco Studios and
AB Video Productions

CD-ROM post-production by Ian Shepherd and Karen Manning at
Sound Recording Technology

This book is produced using paper that is made from wood grown in
managed, sustainable forests. It is natural, renewable and recyclable.
The logging and manufacturing processes conform to the environmental
regulations of the country of origin.

INTRODUCTION

Musical structures is the fourth of six units in the *Music Express Year 7* series. It combines both composing and listening activities to introduce pupils to ternary and rondo form.

This half term unit of work is divided into six coherent and clearly structured lessons. Each lesson is 50 minutes long, with extension activities for schools with more time available, and progresses in a controlled and challenging way.

Pupils are introduced to the principles of musical contrast and unity, which underpin both ternary and rondo form. They listen to, discuss and analyse a wide range of pieces from different genres and periods and apply what they have learnt to composing their own piece of music in ternary form, experimenting with techniques such as beatboxing and rapping. They then perform and evaluate their own work and the work of others against clearly described objectives.

Activities and resources are provided for using acoustic instruments, electronic keyboards and ICT, as suits the needs and set-up of each school.

The activities are described in the book; the CD and CD-ROM provide all the supporting material and resources needed for each lesson.

ABOUT THE AUTHORS OF MUSICAL STRUCTURES

Maureen Hanke MA BMus is the head of Norfolk Education Service. She started her career as a music teacher in the East End of London. Later, as a music adviser, she developed a national reputation for music education workshops and became Head of Music Education at Trinity College of Music. Her work has involved PGCE training, QCA consultation and more recently she devised *Music Express*, an award-winning school resource.

Elizabeth Bray worked for several years as Head of Music at Daventry William Parker School before taking up the post of Advanced Skills Teacher for Music at The Priory LSST in Lincoln, where she is also involved in county initiatives. She has written several articles on music education and worked as an OFSTED inspector.

John Stephens has taught music at all levels for almost twenty years in the London boroughs of Greenwich, Lewisham and Southwark. He has also produced music commercially, acted as a consultant for Lewisham's New Opportunities Fund (NoF) ICT training for secondary music teachers, and is currently Co-ordinator of Greenwich Music Service.

ABOUT THE COMPOSER OF MIND SWAP AND MONTAGUES AND CAPULETS

Rob Bullough (Ekstrak) is a composer and music producer who works mainly with electronic sources. Focussing largely on the more esoteric or 'underground' genres of electronica, he is beginning to carve himself a niche in the world of soundtracks, sound design and music for films and video games. Alongside this, some of Rob's dubstep work is also available on vinyl.

ABOUT MUSIC EXPRESS YEAR 7

Music Express Year 7 provides teaching activities that are imaginative, inspiring and fun. It is user-friendly, well planned, fully resourced and based on good practice for teaching and learning. It promotes inclusion, draws upon a range of music from diverse cultures and enables all pupils to build on their already established skills and knowledge in a purposeful and engaging way.

Each book provides a unit of six weekly lessons, which are intended to be taught over a half term. Each lesson follows the same pattern: objectives are identified and shared with the pupils and the lesson then unfolds through clear activities delivered in a range of styles. The lessons are clearly set out into starter (focus), core activities and plenary, and each lesson provides a suggestion for appropriate homework.

Each lesson is designed to last 50 minutes and approximate timings are provided in the book for each activity.

Suggestions are provided in each lesson for activities which might be used as extension work for students or to extend the lesson for schools with more time available.

This resource offers:

- ways of using a keyboard for appropriate activities;
- ways to incorporate ICT into music teaching and learning;
- extension activities;
- printouts for pupils' files;
- instrumental parts where required;
- all music on CD;
- additional background information on the composers and pieces featured in the activities.

A key feature of the *Music Express Year 7* resource is the use of video clips in which composers and musicians demonstrate and explain their musical thinking. Pupils have the opportunity to reflect on and adopt their thought processes as models for their own learning.

USING MUSIC EXPRESS YEAR 7 AS A SCHEME OF WORK

Music Express Year 7 fulfils the requirements of the Music National Curriculum of England, of Wales and of Northern Ireland and supports the 5-14 National Guidelines for Scotland.

It is inspired and informed by units in the QCA Key Stage 3 scheme of work, but the programmes do not necessarily follow the units exactly. The QCA expectations and lesson objectives are embedded in the units which are designed to enable pupils to meet the standards expected of levels 4 and 5.

The series has been written and created to support high quality teaching and learning and to raise the standards of achievement in music at Key Stage 3. Lessons throughout the unit include reference to:

- the use of evidence and dialogue to identify where pupils are in their musical learning, where they need to go and how best to get there;
- the opportunity for pupils to identify what needs improving and how they can do so;
- peer and self assessment;
- analysis and evaluation of musicians in action to help develop the competence and confidence of every learner;
- clear indication of managing music lessons in a range of whole class, group and individual teaching and learning situations;
- ICT strategies.

Each unit has all the content required for each lesson leaving the teacher to focus on their teaching skills.

THE UNITS

There are six units in *Music Express Year 7*, published as six separate Book + CD + CD-ROM packs. Below is a list of the titles available in the series:

BOOK 1: BRIDGING UNIT (LINKS TO QCA UNIT 1)

Bridging unit is a composing unit that builds on the vast range of musical experiences in Year 6 and is designed, therefore, to help address the wide range of skills, knowledge and understanding that pupils bring to Year 7.

Pupils work initially with simple rhythmic and melodic patterns and, following a workshop style, they use improvisation as a means to composition. Through a commissioned piece of music, pupils listen to and observe the composing process, and in a series of video clips showing an interview with the composer, they gain an insight into his creative thinking. Pupils complete a composition and are able to consider the strengths of their work against clearly described assessment criteria and set their own targets for future learning.

BOOK 2: PERFORMING TOGETHER (PROGRESSES FROM YEAR 5/6 UNIT 20)

This unit develops and demonstrates pupils' ability to prepare and take part in a large group performance. It provides an opportunity for pupils to maintain and develop the invaluable skills of learning by ear, reading simple notation, rehearsing a part and working as an ensemble. All parts are available on the CD and CD-ROM. Principles of preparation unfold throughout the unit and the flexibility of the material provided (eg opportunities for two-part singing, solo spots, improvisation and simple movement/dance routines) ensures that everyone can be included.

The unit is an important foundation for work in arranging and song writing later in the year. It also provides a useful basis for those pupils wanting to start a band or group out of school, who will need to learn how to rehearse and perform the songs they want to play.

BOOK 3: MUSICAL CYCLES (WEST AFRICA) (LINKS TO QCA UNIT 4)

Musical cycles (West Africa) combines performing, listening and composition activities to explore the structures and key characteristics of West African music and its instruments. Teaching and learning are illustrated through video clips and clearly described workshop activities that explore musical cycles, signals and rhythmic and melodic improvisation. Listening is integral to the work and CD extracts include a traditional rhythm from Guinea/Sierra Leone, and recordings of performances by Mamady Keïta and the Malian singer, Oumou Sangaré. The unit unfolds to enable pupils either to complete a composition activity, modelled by a professional composer, or to prepare a performance of *Djolé*.

BOOK 4: MUSICAL STRUCTURES (LINKS TO QCA UNIT 2)

This unit introduces pupils to ternary and rondo form. It employs a combination of composition and listening activities, developing pupils' ability to listen analytically and providing many opportunities for creative practical work.

Pupils learn about the principles of musical contrast which underpin both ternary and rondo form, through listening to and analysing music from different genres and periods. They then apply what they have learnt to compose, perform and evaluate their own piece of music in ternary form, using techniques such as beatboxing and rap.

BOOK 5: ARRANGING MUSIC (LINKS TO QCA UNIT 6)

Building on the *Performing together* unit (*Music Express Year 7 Book 2*) pupils learn about arranging techniques through listening to, arranging and performing a traditional spiritual and an original spiritual-style composition.

Pupils learn about the key tools of arranging, revisiting chords and encountering instrumentation. They are guided through an arrangement and then create their own, enabling them to develop critical judgements on the characteristics both of their own arrangement and those of others.

Musical clichés is the last of the six units – the finale to the *Music Express Year 7* series. The unit develops pupils' ability to recognise, analyse and use a range of musical clichés used in a specific musical genre.

Pupils are introduced to the musical clichés and conventions used in action film music through listening to and analysing extracts from different film soundtracks and completing workshop-style activities based around a piece of music specially composed for the unit. Using the clichés they have learnt, they then compose and perform their own piece of music to fit an extract from a teaser trailer from the blockbuster action film, *Gladiator*.

Please note – we have not included a separate Soundscapes (ICT) unit: instead we have integrated ICT into each unit by offering the opportunity to develop objectives through ICT, electronic keyboards and/or classroom instruments and acoustic instruments.

PREPARATION AND PLANNING

Music Express Year 7 Book 4 is designed to minimise preparation time.

Learning objectives and outcomes are given at the start of each lesson. **Teaching tips** also provide differentiation and assessment, and there is an exemplar lesson plan on the CD-ROM.

The unit and lesson aims are provided on the CD-ROM both in a **presentation** and on printouts for the teacher to view with the pupils. The assessment criteria are also provided as a printout on the CD-ROM.

A complete list of resources is given at the start of each lesson. Key words are highlighted in bold in the activity text when they are first introduced and their definitions are given on each page under **Key words**. There is a glossary at the back of the book and a printout of key words is also provided for pupils on the CD-ROM.

Icons next to the activity headings indicate what you will need to prepare:

Printouts icon: some activities require worksheets or background information to be printed out from the CD-ROM.

Optional printouts icon: for some activities worksheets are suggested but are not essential to the activity.

CD icon: details which audio tracks are required.

Optional CD icon: for some activities audio tracks are suggested but are not essential to the activity.

Video clips icon: you will need to have a computer and data projector set up to show the video clips.

Optional video clips icon: for some activities a video clip is suggested but is not essential to the activity. You will need to have a computer and data projector set up to show the video clips.

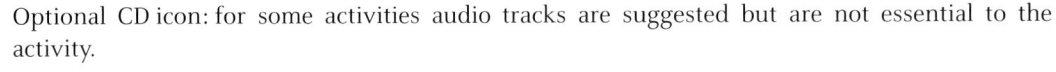 Midi files icon: indicates that midi files are required. You will need to have a midi sequencer installed on your computer, eg Cubasis.

Presentation: you will need to have a computer and data projector or whiteboard set up to show the unit overview and learning intentions for each lesson in a presentation on the CD-ROM.

Other resources required are listed under **Resources** in the book at the start of each lesson.

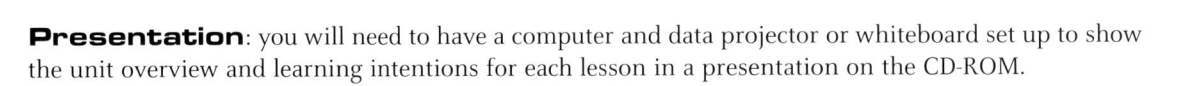

CLASSROOM MANAGEMENT

Music Express Year 7 is designed to enhance and support individual teaching styles. It is not intended to dictate paradigms or pedagogy but rather to make suggestions. Each lesson includes suggestions for managing the activities, including ideas for whole class teaching, small group teaching and giving opportunities to individuals to show leadership and to work on their own. How the activities are managed may need to be adapted to meet the physical environments and cultures of individual schools. Lessons towards the end of each unit expect pupils to demonstrate more independence in the personal management of their learning as the questions and tasks become generally more open.

Each lesson contains many more ideas and much more information than would be expected to be included in a 50-minute teaching period. The lessons are rich in extension activities, alternative keyboard activities, ICT activities and extra background information. When teachers are selecting activities and material, they should bear in mind that all pupils must be able to advance their musical skills, knowledge and understanding. For example it may not be appropriate to give all the background information for all the CD extracts on first using them, as this might interrupt the flow of the lesson. However, the information is available for use at an appropriate point in the unit.

Notation is introduced and used throughout the units in accordance with the lesson objectives and learning outcomes. It is for the teacher to decide if using notation is appropriate for their pupils and to adapt the content of the lesson accordingly, either by increasing the use of conventional notation or by increasing the amount of music learnt by ear.

ASSESSMENT

Music Express Year 7 has several layers of assessment. As an initial support, Teaching tips are provided throughout each lesson. These give further clarification of aspects of the lesson and points that might be of particular benefit to the new teacher. At the end of each lesson there is a summary of points for assessment. These, together with the plenary sessions, combine to provide an ongoing picture of whole class development. They provide an opportunity for the pupils and the teacher to decide what stage the pupils are at in their learning, where they need to go and how best to get there. Major pieces of work towards the end of each unit have an assessment sheet supporting the National Curriculum level descriptions and an opportunity for self, peer and teacher assessment to consider the quality of the work. These build to give a profile of progress for each pupil. Each unit includes an end of unit evaluation that pupils have the opportunity to complete.

SINGING

Music Express Year 7 does not provide instruction on using the voice – however, warm-up exercises and guidance are provided. Do remind pupils to put as little pressure on the throat as possible and instead support the sound with air from the diaphragm. Often pupils sing from the throat – forcing the air in this way can easily lead to cracked notes or neck strain, particularly in the adolescent voice. Singing from the diaphragm should create a warm, rich sound with extensive dynamic possibilities.

It is a common mistake to put less effort into singing quietly. Remind singers to use more air and greater effort to support a quiet note. In this way they will be able to make a quiet note that is both potent and sustained.

Some pupils will find it hard to pitch a note accurately. *Music Express Year 7* frequently uses a call and response format, as it gives pupils less time to worry. Being able to hear a tune in their heads first will also help pupils to vocalise the internal sound correctly.

A warm-up is a useful and important activity to avoid strained voices and to get pupils in the right frame of mind for singing. An effective activity is to use the letter 'F' sound. Take a deep breath and start the sound slowly, gradually quickening, like a steam engine pulling away from the platform. Encourage the pupils to feel the push from their diaphragm and to watch and feel their own stomachs going in and out.

ICT

Many of the activities in *Music Express Year 7* will benefit from the use of a computer and whiteboard to display the supporting materials found on the CD-ROM.

In addition, some activities have specific ICT activities, details of which can be found at the end of each lesson.

Some of the ICT activities are led by the teacher from the front of the class using a whiteboard, for example, using a karaoke player in Books 2 and 5. For these activities, make sure that the computer's sound output is connected to a classroom hi-fi (or equivalent), so that pupils can hear clearly while they clap rhythms or sing.

Some of the ICT activities require pupils to work independently in groups, for example using a midi sequencer in Books 1, 4, 5 and 6. This might make it necessary for the group using the computer to use headphones, if, for example, the rest of the class is working in groups with their instruments in the same area. Some music departments will have more than one computer, in which case teachers may be able to involve more groups in the ICT activities.

All the ICT activities should be deliverable on either a PC or a Mac computer. Software guidance is given on the CD-ROM.

ELECTRONIC KEYBOARDS

Many schools are equipped with electronic keyboards and many pupils will relish the idea of learning to play the keyboard. The keyboard's functions can easily be taught and exploited to achieve musical learning objectives. Laying down the foundations of good technique is an important aspect of Year 7 keyboard work. In *Music Express Year 7* keyboard tuition starts from the very beginning, providing materials to demonstrate good hand positions, emphasising the importance of developing both hands in playing and establishing an understanding of fingering.

One keyboard per pupil is the ideal situation, but if pupils are sharing, ensure that partners swap places regularly.

Each unit provides activities both for the beginner and more confident player, but teachers must remember that each unit has higher expectations of achievement and any pupils who miss the earlier units may miss some important developmental work.

Fingering is suggested throughout the unit, but it can be changed, or at times ignored, if it becomes too much of an impediment to the creative process.

It is not practical to discuss here the many brands and models of keyboard available in such a fast developing market. However, *Music Express Year 7* does assume that the keyboards which schools use will support some basic functions: eg timbre, tempo, style and volume. The facility to record will also be invaluable.

Please note that teaching activity time does not include familiarising yourself with keyboard functionality and ICT software and, depending on experience, you might need to allow extra planning time to do this.

MUSICAL STRUCTURES: OUTLINE

Lesson 1 Musical contrasts

OBJECTIVES

By the end of the lesson pupils should:

- realise the importance of structure in music;
- understand the meaning of ternary form;
- know how contrast and unity are used in musical structures.

OUTCOMES

Pupils:

- are able to identify how contrast and unity are used in musical structures;
- are able to identify the sections of a piece in ternary form;
- compose their own melodic theme and perform it to the class.

Lesson 2 Composing tools

OBJECTIVES

By the end of the lesson pupils should:

- understand how musical themes can be extended;
- understand why looping can be a useful compositional tool.

OUTCOMES

Pupils:

- learn about percussion timbres;
- extend musical themes by looping them.

Lesson 3 Composing an A section

OBJECTIVES

By the end of the lesson pupils should:

- understand how theme, timbre, texture and dynamics can enhance the mood of a composition;
- be able to combine and loop a melodic and rhythmic theme.

OUTCOMES

Pupils:

- compose an A section for their ternary form composition;
- perform their A section to the class.

Lesson 4 Composing a B section

OBJECTIVES

By the end of the lesson pupils should:

- know how to create contrast in a ternary form composition.

OUTCOMES

Pupils:

- learn about rap;
- create a contrasting B section for their ternary form composition.

Lesson 5 Developing and performing

OBJECTIVES

By the end of the lesson pupils should:

- be able to create a convincing ending;
- understand the purpose of writing down a musical structure.

OUTCOMES

Pupils:

- complete their ternary form composition;
- perform their ternary form composition to the class;
- assess and evaluate their own and other pupils' compositions.

Lesson 6 Rondo form

OBJECTIVES

By the end of the lesson pupils should:

- recognise the relationship and differences between ternary and rondo form;
- understand the meaning of the term rondo form.

OUTCOMES

Pupils:

- learn about rondo form;
- identify and discuss musical structures;
- consolidate their understanding of ternary and rondo form.

Lesson 1 Musical contrasts

Focus

1	Pupils learn about unity and contrast in music	>> KEYBOARD
2	Pupils learn about texture and timbre	>> KEYBOARD >> ICT
3	Pupils learn about thematic contrast	>> KEYBOARD >> ICT
4	Pupils compose a musical theme	>> KEYBOARD >> ICT

Plenary

Lesson 2 Composing tools

Focus

1	Introduce the melodic themes in *Ideas bank A*	>> KEYBOARD >> ICT
2	Introduce percussion timbres	>> KEYBOARD >> ICT
3	Introduce the rhythmic themes in *Ideas bank A*	>> KEYBOARD >> ICT
4	Pupils learn about looping	>> KEYBOARD >> ICT

Plenary

Lesson 3 Composing an A section

Focus

1	Pupils choose a rhythmic theme for their A section	>> KEYBOARD >> ICT
2	Pupils add a melodic theme to their A section	>> KEYBOARD >> ICT
3	Pupils complete their A section	>> KEYBOARD >> ICT
4	Pupils perform their A section to the class	

Plenary

Lesson 4 Composing a B section

Focus

1	Introduce *Ideas bank B*	>> KEYBOARD >> ICT
2	Pupils choose a theme from *Ideas bank B*	>> KEYBOARD >> ICT
3	Introduce rap	>> KEYBOARD
4	Pupils develop their B section	>> KEYBOARD >> ICT

Plenary

Lesson 5 Developing and performing

Focus

1	Pupils create their final A section	>> KEYBOARD >> ICT
2	Pupils compose an ending for their composition	>> KEYBOARD >> ICT
3	Pupils practise their composition	>> KEYBOARD >> ICT
4	Pupils perform their composition to the class	

Plenary

Lesson 6 Rondo form

Focus

1	Introduce rondo form	>> ICT
2	Pupils analyse *Quadrille*	>> ICT
3	Pupils demonstrate their knowledge of ternary and rondo form	

Plenary

Musical contrasts

OBJECTIVES

By the end of the lesson pupils should:

■ realise the importance of structure in music;

■ understand the meaning of ternary form;

■ know how contrast and unity are used in musical structures.

OUTCOMES

Pupils:

□ are able to identify how contrast and unity are used in musical structures;

□ are able to identify the sections of a piece in ternary form;

□ compose their own melodic theme and perform it to the class.

RESOURCES

AUDIO CD
Tracks 1–4

CD-ROM
• Presentation
• Printouts 1–8
• Teacher information (optional)
• Midi files (optional)

INSTRUMENTS
• Untuned and tuned instruments (optional)
• Electronic keyboards (optional)

ICT
• Whiteboard or computer with data projector and sound
• Midi sequencer software (optional)

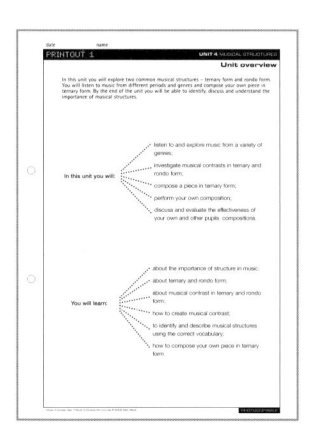

Printout 1: Unit overview

Printout 2: Learning intentions lessons 1–6

Focus

5 mins 1 2 **Presentation**

■ Introduce this unit using the presentation on the CD-ROM or printout 1.

■ Define the term **musical structure** and brainstorm as a class the reasons why pupils think structure is important in music *(eg structure makes music easier to understand. A good musical structure should take the listener on a musical journey from beginning to middle to end).*

■ Display the learning intentions for this lesson using the presentation on the CD-ROM or printout 2.

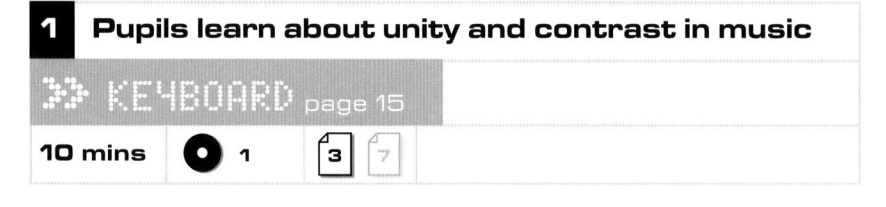

1 **Pupils learn about unity and contrast in music**

》》 KEYBOARD page 15

10 mins ● 1 3 7

■ Play track 1 (*A fifth of Beethoven* by Walter Murphy, from the film *Saturday Night Fever*) and discuss as a class how the composer has created contrast and unity in the music. *(Different instruments, rhythms and melodies are used throughout and the music is not always the same volume. However, the opening melody keeps recurring, particularly at the end, which gives a sense of unity to the music.)*

■ Distribute copies of *Musical contrasts* (printout 3) and define the term **musical contrast**, explaining that the two most important features of a musical structure are contrast and unity.

■ Play track 1 again and ask if anyone can work out how many sections there are in *A fifth of Beethoven (three),* by listening out for musical contrasts, such as different melodies, moods, instruments or dynamics.

■ Explain that *A fifth of Beethoven* uses a musical structure called ternary form and that musical structures can be described using letter names: each section that sounds similar is given the same letter. Define **ternary form**.

TEACHING TIPS

More information about ternary form is given on *Ternary form – background information* (printout 7), which pupils will use later this lesson.

As it is not expected that pupils will recognise tonal contrast aurally, this book focusses on other ways of creating musical contrast.

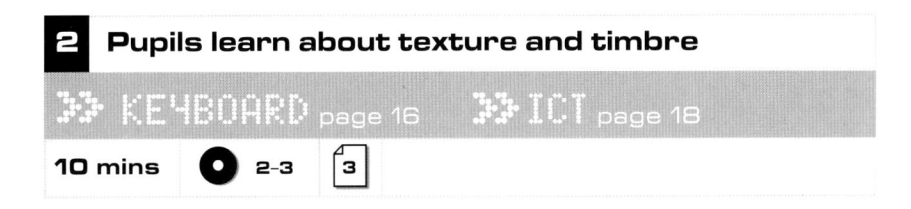

2 **Pupils learn about texture and timbre**

KEYBOARD page 16   **ICT** page 18

10 mins ● 2-3 3

- Using *Musical contrasts* (printout 3), define the terms **timbre** and **texture**.

- Play track 2 (*A fifth of Beethoven – A section*). Discuss as a class which timbres are used in this extract *(drum kit, guitars, strings, trombone, bass guitar)*.

- Play track 3 (*A fifth of Beethoven – B section*). Discuss which timbres are used in this extract and compare these with the timbres used in track 2 *(drum kit, guitars, strings, trombone, bass guitar are used in track 2, but track 3 also uses a vibraslap, horn, trumpets and hammond organ. We can therefore say that the timbres contrast with each other between sections)*.

- Using tracks 2 and 3, discuss how the texture varies between the A and B sections of *A fifth of Beethoven*. *(The A section has a thick texture, created mostly by the use of sustained string sounds. The B section has a thinner texture at first, with drums, vibraslap, bass and guitars, but the texture gradually thickens when the hammond organ and strings are introduced.)*

TEACHING TIP
You might need to help pupils to identify some of the timbres used in *A fifth of Beethoven*.

KEY WORDS

musical structure – the way in which musical ideas are ordered. Musical structures are given different names, eg ternary, rondo.

musical contrast – differences in how music sounds. Contrast can be created by varying dynamics, texture, timbre and other musical factors.

ternary form – a piece of music in three sections: the first and third sections are similar and the second section is different. Ternary form is also known as ABA form.

timbre – the unique characteristic sound of each instrument. Every instrument, including the human voice, has its own particular sound.

texture – the number of parts or performers in a piece. Some pieces are written for a set number of parts or performers and these create particular textures, eg solo, duet, trio, quartet and quintet.

accent – a symbol in written music, which tells the performer to play an individual note with special emphasis.

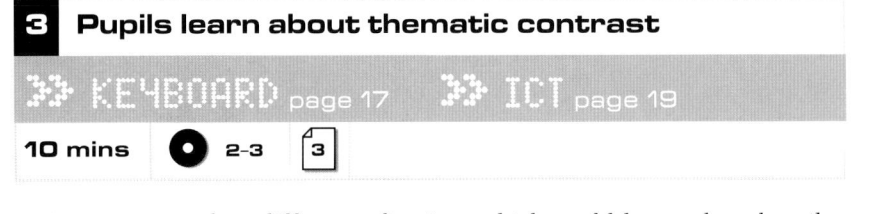

3 **Pupils learn about thematic contrast**

KEYBOARD page 17   **ICT** page 19

10 mins ● 2-3 3

- Brainstorm as a class different adjectives which could be used to describe mood *(eg calm, exciting, dramatic, lazy, triumphant, mournful, hypnotic)*.

- Draw pupils attention to the melodies on *Musical contrasts* (printout 3) and explain that these melodies are from Beethoven's *Fifth symphony*, upon which *A fifth of Beethoven* is based.

- Explain the term **accent** and that the marks underneath the notes of the first melody are accents.

- Play the melodies on printout 3 (see below) and ask pupils to describe what mood each melody creates and how *(eg the first melody uses a mixture of short and long accented notes and sounds threatening. The second melody sounds more relaxed, because it uses even note lengths and has no accents)*.

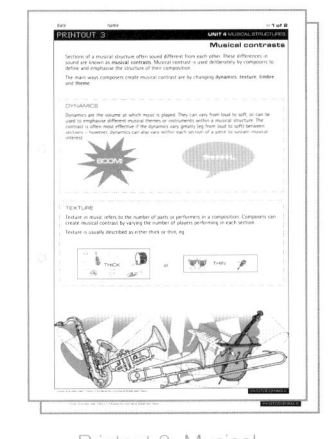

Printout 3: Musical contrasts (2 pages)

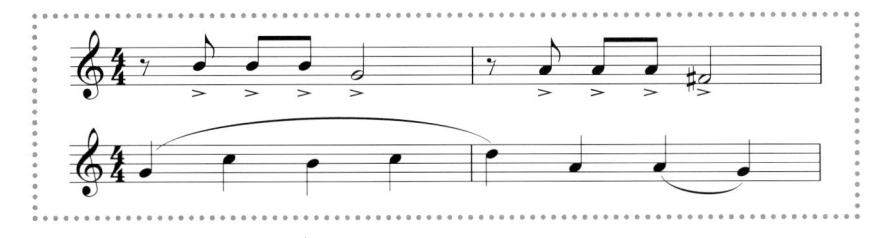

KEY WORDS

theme – a musical idea, which is an important element in the structure of a piece of music. Different themes can create different moods.

ASSESSMENT FOR LEARNING

• Who can successfully identify and discuss contrasts within a piece of music?

• Who can use the new terminology in response to questions?

• Who understands the importance of musical structure?

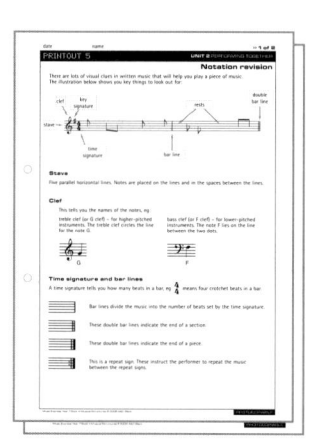

Printout 5: Notation revision
(2 pages)

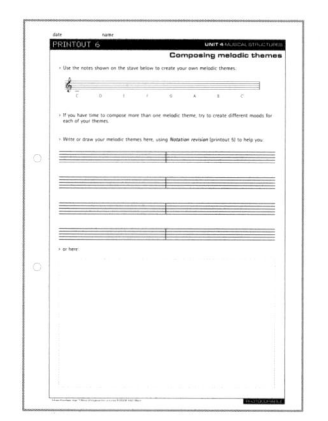

Printout 6: Composing melodic themes

■ Explain that:

• the most common method of creating contrast in a musical structure is to create a different mood in each section;

• composers often use different melodies and rhythms to create these different moods and we call these melodies and rhythms musical themes.

■ Define the term **theme** and listen to tracks 2 and 3 again, discussing as a class how the moods of the string theme in the A section and the guitar theme in the B section contrast with each other. *(The string theme in the A section sounds scary and threatening. The guitar theme in the B section sounds funky.)*

TEACHING TIPS

Pupils often describe mood as being either 'fast' or 'slow'. Explain that mood describes the feeling that music creates, rather than the speed at which it is played.

Be prepared for pupils to give different answers when describing the mood the themes create. Always encourage pupils to explain the reasons for the answer they give.

The melodic themes on printout 3 have been transposed from the original key (C minor) to facilitate playing.

You might like to play Beethoven's *Fifth symphony* to put the themes on printout 3 in context, if you have a recording available.

4   Pupils compose a musical theme

KEYBOARD page 18   **ICT** page 19

10 mins   ● 4   [5] [6]

■ Divide the class into pairs and distribute any tuned instruments you have available amongst the pupils. Explain that each pair should compose a melodic theme, using *Notation revision* (printout 5) and *Composing melodic themes* (printout 6) to help them.

■ Encourage pupils to consider what mood their theme will create and how the timbre(s) they have available could emphasise or dictate this mood.

■ When pupils have composed their theme, invite as many pairs as possible to perform their theme to the class and discuss as a class whether each pair was successful in creating the mood they intended.

EXTENSION ACTIVITY

Pupils compose a second melodic theme, which contrasts in mood with the first theme they composed.

TEACHING TIPS

If you prefer, you could ask pupils to experiment with improvising short contrasting melodic themes using their voices or any tuned instruments you have available, while you tap a steady pulse.

You might like to play track 4 (*Ideas bank A – melodic theme 1*) to demonstrate the kind of theme pupils could compose.

Plenary

5 mins

- Discuss as a class the quote 'Music makes you feel a feeling' (Edgar Harburg), referring in particular to the music that pupils have listened to, composed and performed this lesson.

- Ask pupils whether they think there is any purpose to music other than to 'make you feel a feeling' *(eg playing music brings people together, listening to music can help you relax, music is sometimes used for celebratory occasions).*

Homework 7

- Pupils research the history of ternary form using *Ternary form – background information* (printout 7).

KEYBOARD (see page 12)

1 Pupils learn about unity and contrast in music

10 mins ● 1 [4] [7]

- Play track 1 (*A fifth of Beethoven* by Walter Murphy, from the film *Saturday night fever*) and discuss as a class how the composer has created contrast and unity in the music. *(Different instruments, rhythms and melodies are used throughout and the music is not always the same volume. However, the opening melody keeps recurring, particularly at the end, which gives a sense of unity to the music.)*

- Distribute copies of *Musical contrasts – keyboard* (printout 4) and define the term **musical contrast**, explaining that the two most important features of a musical structure are contrast and unity.

- Play track 1 again and ask if anyone can work out how many sections there are in *A fifth of Beethoven (three).*

- Explain that *A fifth of Beethoven* uses a musical structure called ternary form and that musical structures can be described using letter names: each section that sounds similar is given the same letter. Define **ternary form**.

TEACHING TIPS

More information about ternary form is given on *Ternary form – background information* (printout 7), which pupils will use later this lesson.

As it is not expected that pupils will recognise tonal contrast aurally, this book focusses on other ways of creating musical contrast.

◄◄ RETURN TO ACTIVITY 2 (page 13)

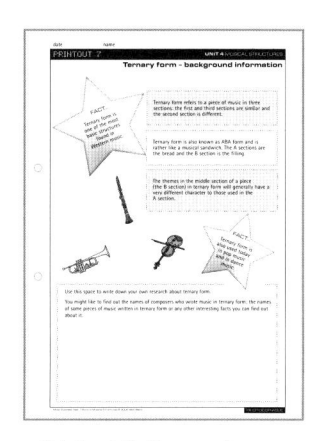

Printout 7: Ternary form –
background information

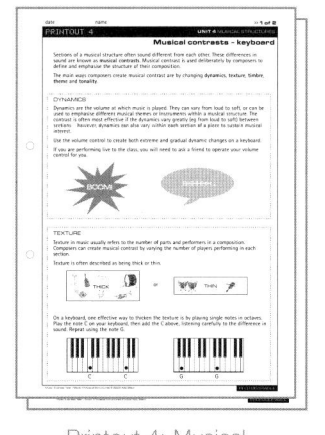

Printout 4: Musical
contrasts – keyboard
(2 pages)

KEYBOARD (see page 13)

2 **Pupils learn about texture and timbre**

10 mins ● 2-3 [4]

- Using *Musical contrasts – keyboard* (printout 4), define the terms **timbre** and **texture**.

- Explain that the different timbres on a keyboard are often called voices and that these voices are usually grouped into different categories, such as woodwind, brass and strings.

- Make sure pupils know how to change the voice on their keyboards (select VOICE and the number of the instrument you require).

- Play track 2 (*A fifth of Beethoven – A section*). Discuss as a class which timbres are used in this extract *(drum kit, guitars, strings, trombone, bass guitar)* and help pupils familiarise themselves with the sound of these timbres on their keyboards.

- Play track 3 (*A fifth of Beethoven – B section*). Discuss which timbres are used in this extract and compare these with the timbres used in track 2 *(drum kit, guitars, strings, trombone, bass guitar are used in track 2, but track 3 also uses a vibraslap, horn, trumpets and hammond organ. We can therefore say that the timbres contrast with each other between sections).*

- Using tracks 2 and 3, discuss how the texture varies between the A and B sections of *A fifth of Beethoven. (The A section has a thick texture, created mostly by the use of sustained string sounds. The B section has a thinner texture at first, with drums, vibraslap, bass and guitars, but the texture gradually thickens when the hammond organ and strings are introduced.)*

TEACHING TIPS

You might need to help pupils to identify some of the timbres used in *A fifth of Beethoven*.

For more information on selecting voices, see *Using electronic keyboards* in the Teacher information section of the CD-ROM.

◀◀ RETURN TO ACTIVITY 3 (page 13)

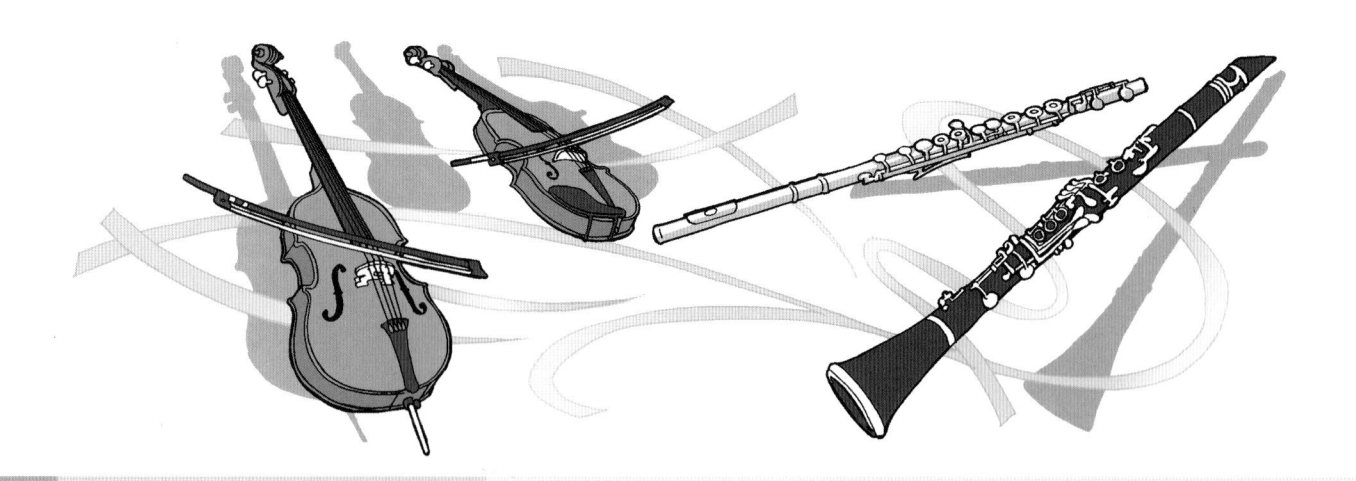

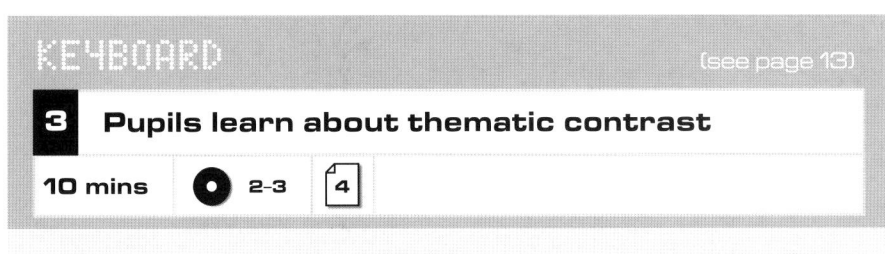

- Brainstorm as a class different adjectives which could be used to describe mood *(eg calm, exciting, dramatic, lazy, triumphant, mournful, hypnotic).*

- Draw pupils attention to the melodies on *Musical contrasts – keyboard* (printout 4) and explain that these melodies are from Beethoven's *Fifth symphony*, upon which *A fifth of Beethoven* is based.

- Explain the term **accent** and that the marks underneath the notes of the first melody are accents.

- Ensure pupils know how to change voices on their keyboard. Play the themes on printout 4 (see below) and ask pupils to repeat them after you on their keyboards, using a string timbre for the first theme and a woodwind timbre for the second theme.

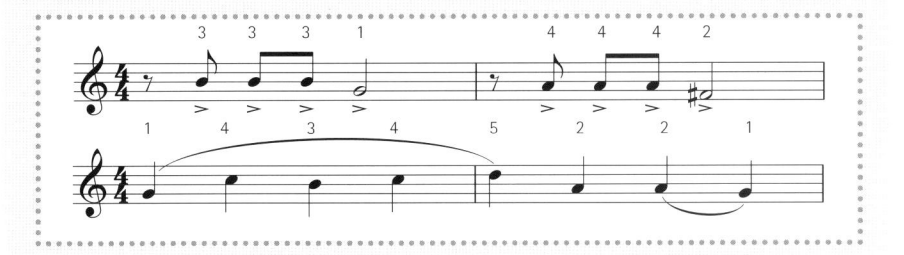

- Ask pupils to describe what mood each creates and how *(eg the first theme uses a mixture of short and long accented notes and sounds threatening. The second theme sounds more relaxed, because it uses even note lengths and has no accents).*

- Explain that:
  - the most common method of creating contrast in a musical structure is to create a different mood in each section;
  - composers often use different melodies and rhythms to create these different moods and we call these melodies and rhythms musical themes.

- Define the term **theme** and listen to tracks 2 and 3 again, discussing as a class how the moods of the string theme in the A section and the guitar theme in the B section contrast with each other. *(The string theme in the A section sounds scary and threatening. The guitar theme in the B section sounds funky.)*

TEACHING TIPS

Pupils often describe mood as being either 'fast' or 'slow'. Explain that mood describes the feeling that music creates, rather than the speed at which it is played.

Be prepared for pupils to give different answers when describing the mood the themes create. Always encourage pupils to explain the reasons for the answer they give.

The melodic themes on printout 4 have been transposed from the original key (C minor) to facilitate playing.

If sharing a keyboard, both pupils should play using their right hand, two octaves apart.

You might like to play Beethoven's *Fifth symphony* to put the themes on printout 4 in context, if you have a recording available.

◀◀ RETURN TO ACTIVITY 4   (page 14)

KEYBOARD (see page 14)

4 **Pupils compose a musical theme**

10 mins 4 5 6

- Distribute copies of *Notation revision* (printout 5) and *Composing melodic themes* (printout 6) and introduce the task, as described on page 14.

- Encourage pupils to consider what mood their theme will create and how the timbre(s) they have available could emphasise or dictate this mood.

- When pupils have composed their theme, invite as many pairs as possible to perform their theme to the class and discuss as a class whether each pair was successful in creating the mood they intended.

EXTENSION ACTIVITY

Pupils compose a second melodic theme, which contrasts in mood with the first theme they composed.

TEACHING TIPS

If you prefer, you could ask pupils to experiment with improvising short contrasting melodic themes using their keyboards, while you tap a steady pulse.

You might like to play track 4 (*Ideas bank A – melodic theme 1*) to demonstrate the kind of theme pupils could compose.

Pupils could work individually at their keyboards, if resources allow.

◀◀ RETURN TO PLENARY (page 15)

ICT (see page 13)

2 **Pupils learn about texture and timbre**

10 mins 3 MIDI

- Before starting this activity, load the file *ternary.mid* into the sequencer and make sure that it can be heard clearly over the computer's sound system (see *Using a midi sequencer* in the Teacher information section of the CD-ROM for further information).

- Play *ternary.mid* and explain that this is another piece of music in ternary form. Encourage pupils to follow the music in the arrange window as it plays.

- Using *Musical contrasts* (printout 3), explain the terms **timbre** and **texture**.

- Play the file again and discuss how the timbres and textures contrast in the music. *(The piece begins with a bass instrument and later features synthesisers. The B section introduces sustained string sounds and the final passage uses bells, which emphasise the melody. The texture of the opening is very thin, but it gradually thickens when the synthesisers enter. The texture of the B section is thin once again, and the texture of the final A section is thickened by the addition of bells.)*

◀◀ RETURN TO ACTIVITY 3 (page 13)

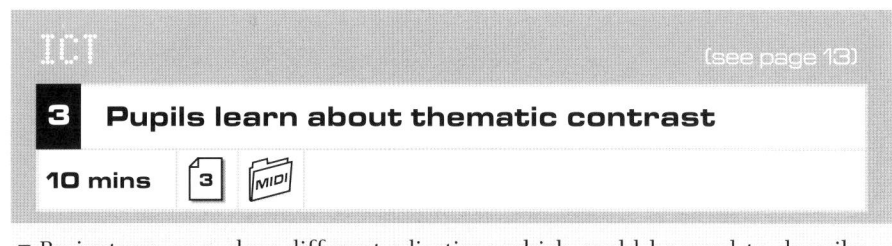

(see page 13)

3 Pupils learn about thematic contrast

10 mins 3 MIDI

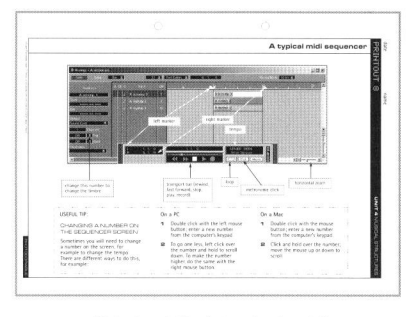

Printout 8: A typical midi sequencer

- Brainstorm as a class different adjectives which could be used to describe mood *(eg calm, exciting, dramatic, lazy, triumphant, mournful, hypnotic).*

- Using *Musical contrasts* (printout 3), explain the term **theme** and that themes can either be melodic or just rhythmic.

- Explain that the most common method of creating contrast in a musical structure is to use different themes to create a different mood in each section.

- Play bars 13–23 of *ternary.mid* and ask pupils to describe the mood the bass theme and the string theme create and how *(eg the bass theme uses short notes and sounds exciting, but the string theme uses long notes and sounds relaxed).*

RETURN TO ACTIVITY 4 (page 14)

ICT (see page 14)

4 Pupils compose a musical theme

10 mins 8 MIDI

- Before starting this activity, load the file *ideas.mid* into the sequencer and create a new track with the patch number configured to a woodwind sound. (See *Using a midi sequencer* in the Teacher information section of the CD-ROM for further information.)

- Distribute copies of *A typical midi sequencer* (printout 8) and ensure that pupils are familiar with how to input notes into the key edit window using the cursor tools and how to change the timbre of a track by altering the patch number.

- Explain that pupils should:
  - compose their own short melodic theme by inputting notes into the key edit window using the cursor tools;
  - only use the notes C, D, E, F, G, A and B and make their theme approximately two bars long;
  - experiment with changing the timbre of the track to emphasise the kind of mood their theme creates.

- Listen back to the theme and discuss as a class how effectively it portrays the intended mood.

EXTENSION ACTIVITY
Pupils compose a second musical theme, which contrasts in mood with the first theme they composed.

TEACHING TIP
For help using the cursor tools and changing patch numbers, see *Using a midi sequencer* in the Teacher information section of the CD-ROM.

RETURN TO PLENARY (page 15)

Lesson 2

Composing tools

OBJECTIVES

By the end of the lesson pupils should:

■ understand how musical themes can be extended;

■ understand why looping can be a useful compositional tool.

OUTCOMES

Pupils:

☐ learn about percussion timbres;

☐ extend musical themes by looping them.

RESOURCES

AUDIO CD
Tracks 4–18

CD-ROM
• Presentation
• Video clips 1–4
• Printouts 2, 7–13
• Midi files (optional)
• Teacher information (optional)

INSTRUMENTS
• Untuned and tuned instruments (optional)
• Electronic keyboards (optional)

ICT
• Whiteboard or computer with data projector and sound
• Midi sequencer software (optional)

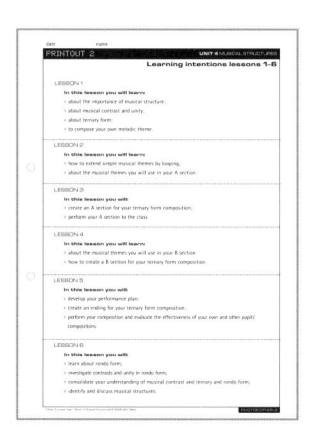

Printout 2: Learning intentions lessons 1–6

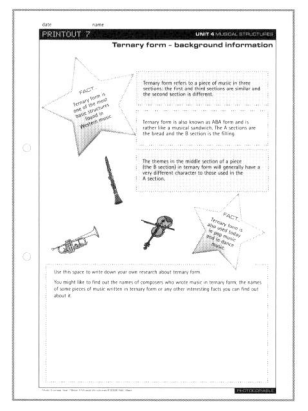

Printout 7: Ternary form – background information

Focus

| 5 mins | 2 7 | Presentation |

■ Revise the meaning of ternary form *(a piece of music in three sections)* and discuss pupils' research about ternary form, which they did for homework, using the notes they made on *Ternary form – background information* (printout 7).

■ Explain the learning intentions for this lesson using the presentation on the CD-ROM or printout 2.

1 Introduce the melodic themes in Ideas bank A

>> KEYBOARD page 22   >> ICT page 25

| 10 mins | ● 4–7 | 9 |

■ Distribute copies of *Ideas bank A* (printout 9) and explain that pupils will use the themes on this printout to compose an A section for their piece in ternary form.

■ Play the melodic themes on printout 9 yourself, or use tracks 4–7 (*Ideas bank A – melodic themes 1–4*), encouraging pupils to follow the notation on the printout as they listen. After each theme, ask pupils to:

• first, clap the rhythm of the theme;
• then, sing along with the theme while you play the track again.

■ Discuss as a class the mood pupils think each theme creates.

TEACHING TIP

The melodic themes on *Ideas bank A* have been notated in a variety of ways, so that you can choose the most appropriate notation for your pupils.

2 Introduce percussion timbres

>> KEYBOARD page 23   >> ICT page 26

| 10 mins | 🎥 1–3 | ● 8 | 11 |

■ Play *Overture* by Killa Kela (track 8) and ask if anyone knows the name of the technique used to perform the percussion sounds *(beatboxing)*.

- Define the term **beatboxing** and explain that beatboxing can be a useful and exciting way of performing percussion sounds.

- Distribute copies of *Beatboxing* (printout 11) and go through it with the class, using video clips 1–3 to learn the kick drum, snare drum and hi-hat sounds, encouraging pupils to practise the sounds after they have watched each clip.

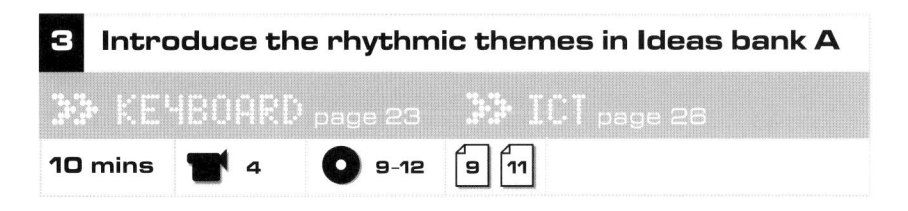

3 **Introduce the rhythmic themes in Ideas bank A**

>> KEYBOARD page 23   >> ICT page 26

10 mins   🎥 4   ⬤ 9–12   [9] [11]

- Display the rhythmic themes on *Ideas bank A* (printout 9) and explain that pupils could either beatbox these themes in their composition or perform them on more traditional percussion instruments, such as a drum kit.

- Play video clip 4 (*Ideas bank A – beatboxed*) to show pupils how these rhythmic themes could be beatboxed, encouraging them to follow the beatbox notation on printout 9 as they listen.

- After each theme, pause the video clip and revise as a class the sounds which are used in the theme. Then, beatbox each theme slowly.

- Play tracks 9–12 (*Ideas bank A – rhythmic themes 1–4*) and listen to how the themes sound when played on a drum kit.

- Discuss as a class the advantages and disadvantages of performing the rhythmic themes on a drum kit and beatboxing them *(eg beatboxing is not as loud as using a drum kit, unless a microphone is used. Drum kits can produce several sounds at once, but beatboxing cannot. However, beatboxing requires no expensive instruments and it is portable and accessible to almost everyone).*

TEACHING TIPS

The rhythmic themes on *Ideas bank A* have been notated in a variety of ways, so that you can choose the most appropriate notation for your pupils.

Ensure pupils have copies of *Beatboxing* (printout 11) to hand as they work.

4 **Pupils learn about looping**

>> KEYBOARD page 24   >> ICT page 27

10 mins   ⬤ 13–18   [9] [11] [13]

- Explain the terms **looping** and **dance music** and that looping is:

  • often used in popular music because it is a useful way of creating a strong rhythmic feel which is easy to dance to;

  • also used in classical music by contemporary composers such as Philip Glass and Steve Reich.

- Distribute copies of *Mind swap – listening sheet* (printout 13) and play *Mind swap* (track 13), explaining that this piece is made up of lots of looped musical themes and that some of these themes are shown on the printout.

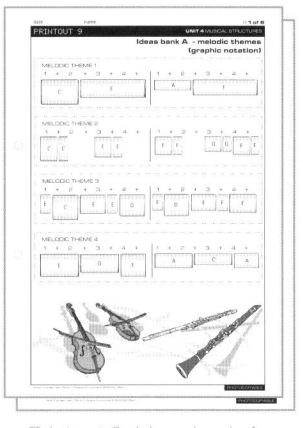

Printout 9: Ideas bank A
(6 pages)

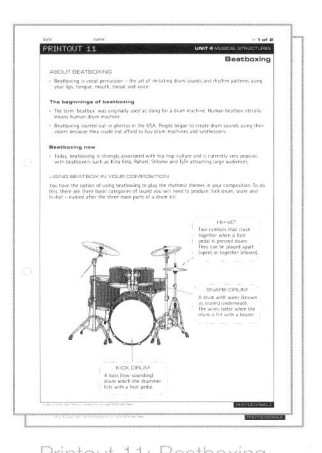

Printout 11: Beatboxing
(2 pages)

ASSESSMENT FOR LEARNING

- Who demonstrates an ability to memorise a musical theme?
- Who can loop musical themes at a steady tempo?
- Who understands why looping can be a useful compositional tool?

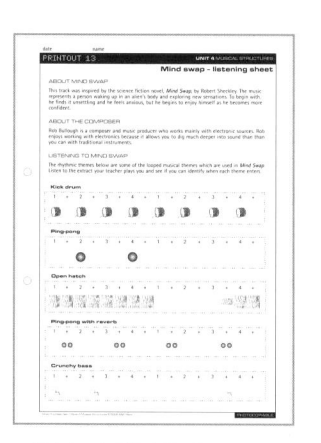

Printout 13: Mind swap – listening sheet

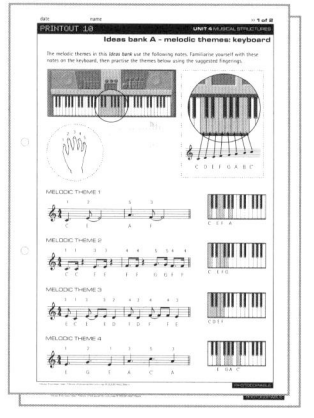

Printout 10: Ideas bank A – keyboard (2 pages)

- Listen to tracks 14–18 (themes from *Mind swap*) and encourage pupils to follow the notation on printout 13 as they listen.

- Play track 13 again as many times as necessary and this time ask pupils to identify when each looped musical theme begins, using printout 13 to help them. Discuss the answers as a class.

EXTENSION ACTIVITY

Pupils experiment with looping themes from *Ideas bank A* (printout 9) using their voices or any tuned or untuned instruments they have available. They may find it useful to have copies of *Beatboxing* (printout 11) to hand as they work.

Plenary

5 mins

- Discuss with the class the effect that looping has on a listener and why looping could be a useful compositional tool *(eg the repetition of a musical theme has a trance-like, hypnotic effect and helps a short musical theme, which might otherwise have been forgotten, stay in the listener's memory. Looping also allows a composer to extend a short musical theme to fill a longer passage)*.

Homework 9 10 11

- Encourage pupils to continue practising the themes from *Ideas bank A*, using their voices or any instruments they have at home and printouts 9–11.

- Ask pupils to bring in any tuned or untuned instruments they have at home to the next lesson, as they will be useful for their composition task.

KEYBOARD   (see page 20)

1 **Introduce the melodic themes in Ideas bank A**

10 mins ● 4–7 10

- Distribute copies of *Ideas bank A – keyboard* (printout 10) and introduce the task as described on page 20.

- Demonstrate the melodic themes on printout 10 yourself, or use tracks 4–7 (*Ideas bank A – melodic themes 1–4*), explaining which notes and fingering to use. Ask pupils to repeat each theme on their keyboard after you have played it.

- Pupils familiarise themselves with the melodic themes using their keyboards.

TEACHING TIP

Circulate round the class as they work and help pupils practise in time to a steady pulse.

RETURN TO ACTIVITY 2   (page 20)

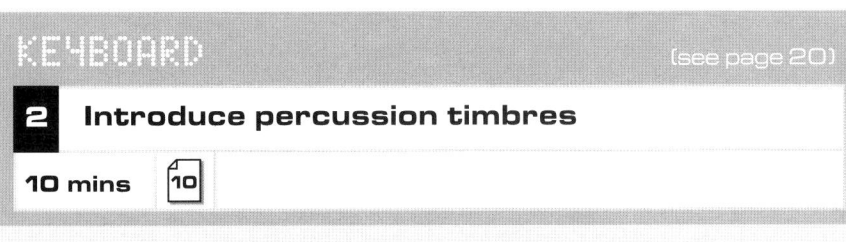

KEYBOARD   (see page 20)

2 **Introduce percussion timbres**

10 mins

- Explain that the rhythmic themes on *Ideas bank A – keyboard* (printout 10) should be performed using the drum kit voice. Demonstrate how to select VOICE then DRUM KIT.

- Ask pupils if anyone knows which instruments make up a drum kit *(kick drum, snare drum, hi-hat, crash cymbal, ride cymbal and tom-toms).*

- Explain that the three most frequently used instruments in a drum kit are the kick drum, snare drum and hi-hat and that these are the instruments pupils will use in their composition.

- Tell pupils that each key in the drum kit voice creates a different sound. Refer them to the illustrations at the base of each key and ask if anyone can find the keys that create the kick drum, snare drum and open and closed hi-hat sounds, using the illustrations to help them.

- Explain that pupils will use these sounds in their composition and that they should now familiarise themselves with these sounds and the keys that produce them.

TEACHING TIP
Consult your keyboard manual for more information on which keys create the kick drum, snare drum and hi-hat sounds on your particular model of keyboard.

◀◀ RETURN TO ACTIVITY 3   (page 21)

KEYBOARD   (see page 21)

3 **Introduce the rhythmic themes in Ideas bank A**

10 mins ● 9-12 [10]

- Display the rhythmic themes on *Ideas bank A – keyboard* (printout 10) and explain their notation using the diagrams on the printout.

- Demonstrate the rhythmic themes yourself, or use tracks 9–12 (*Ideas bank A – melodic themes 1–4*) explaining which keys to use and suggesting suitable fingerings.

- Help pupils familiarise themselves with the rhythmic themes and fingerings using their keyboards.

TEACHING TIPS
If you prefer, you could teach pupils the rhythmic themes aurally before introducing rhythmic notation.
Circulate round the class as they work and help them with the fingerings, if required.

◀◀ RETURN TO ACTIVITY 4   (page 21)

KEYBOARD (see page 21)

4 Pupils learn about looping

10 mins | 13 | 10

- Play *Mind swap* (track 13) and ask pupils if they can work out how it has been constructed *(it is made up of lots of musical themes which are repeated over and over).*

- Explain the term **looping** and that looping is:
  - often used in popular music because it is a useful way of creating a strong rhythmic feel which is easy to dance to;
  - also used in classical music by contemporary composers such as Philip Glass and Steve Reich.

- Show pupils how to use the repeat play function, if there is one, and tell them that this is a simple way of looping a musical theme electronically.

- Ensure pupils have copies of *Ideas bank A – keyboard* (printout 10) and explain that they will now loop a rhythmic theme from *Ideas bank A*. Pupils:
  - choose a rhythmic theme from *Ideas bank A,* which they can play confidently, and record it into the keyboard memory, if keyboards allow;
  - use the repeat play function to listen to the theme looping electronically.

EXTENSION ACTIVITY

Discuss with pupils the advantages of looping a musical theme live compared to looping it electronically *(eg it can be difficult to maintain a steady tempo when looping a theme live, but playing live enables the performer to give more expression to their performance. Electronic looping is quick and simple and makes it easy for composers to create long pieces of music at the touch of a button, but the expression associated with live performance can be lost).*

TEACHING TIPS

To help pupils record their theme into the keyboard memory at a steady tempo, suggest they set their keyboard metronome to a tempo of 80 bpm.

To use the repeat play function, record a theme into a user area (hold down RECORD and track 1). Press stop when you are finished. Press the start button and the keyboard will keep looping that idea until you press stop again. (There may be a slight delay before the repeated theme plays.) Some models of keyboard may differ and require the player to keep pressing the start button to activate the recorded theme.

If your model of keyboard does not have the facility to record, pupils will need to practise looping their chosen rhythmic theme live.

◀◀ RETURN TO PLENARY (page 22)

ICT (see page 20)

1 Introduce the melodic themes in Ideas bank A

10 mins [8] [12] [MIDI]

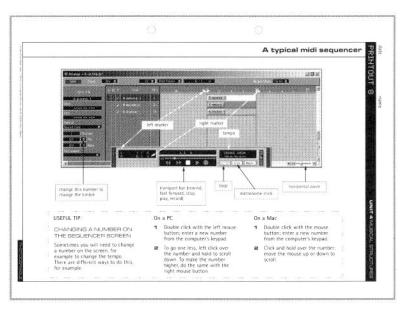

Printout 8: A typical midi sequencer

- Before starting this activity, load the file *ideas.mid* into the sequencer and make sure that it can be heard clearly over the computer's sound system (see *Using a midi sequencer* in the Teacher information section of the CD-ROM for more information). Check that all the parts are muted.

- Distribute copies of *A typical midi sequencer* (printout 8) and *Composing an A section using a midi sequencer* (printout 12) and introduce the task as described on page 20.

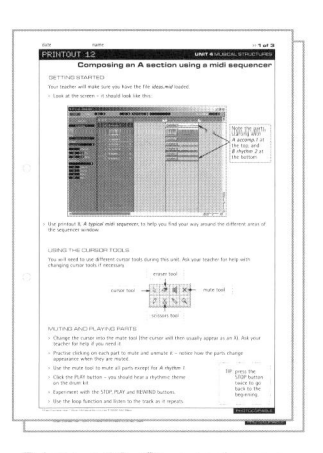

Printout 12: Composing an A section using a midi sequencer (3 pages)

- Explain to the group that the midi file contains eight different themes for them to use in their composition, four of which are melodic and the others are purely rhythmic.

- Explain that pupils will now listen to the themes *A melody 1* and *2* and *A accomp. 1* and *2*.

- Ensure that pupils are familiar with the transport bar and that they can start, stop, pause and play from the beginning. Demonstrate how to unmute the part labelled *A accomp. 1*. Click PLAY and listen to this part on its own.

- Pupils then mute this part and unmute the next one, *A accomp.2*. They follow this process until they have listened to each of the *accomp.* and *melody* parts in isolation.

- Discuss as a class what mood pupils think each theme creates.

TEACHING TIP
Explain that pupils should restrict themselves to the themes prefixed with an A. They will use the themes prefixed with a B later in the unit.

◄◄ RETURN TO ACTIVITY 2 (page 20)

ICT (see page 20)

2 **Introduce percussion timbres**

10 mins [MIDI]

- Open *ideas.mid* in the arrange window and draw pupils' attention to the patch number box at the side of each track.

- Remind pupils that this box lets you change the timbre of a track by inputting a number which relates to a specific timbre.

- Tell pupils that the rhythmic themes in *ideas.mid* have been set up to use the drum kit timbre and that every note in this timbre creates a different sound.

- Ask pupils if anyone knows which instruments make up a drum kit *(kick drum, snare drum, hi-hat, crash cymbal, ride cymbal and tom-toms)*.

- Explain that the three most frequently used instruments in a drum kit are the kick drum, snare drum and hi-hat and that these are the instruments pupils will use in their composition.

- Select *A rhythm 1* and open it in the key edit window. Draw pupils' attention to the keyboard at the left of the window and show pupils which notes create the kick drum, snare drum and open and closed hi-hat sounds by pressing play and encouraging them to follow the music as it progresses.

TEACHING TIP
Consult your sequencer manual for more information on which notes create the kick drum, snare drum and hi-hat sounds on your particular type of sequencer.

◀◀ RETURN TO ACTIVITY 3 (page 21)

ICT (see page 21)

3 **Introduce the rhythmic themes in Ideas bank A**

10 mins [12] [MIDI]

- Explain that pupils should now listen to the rhythmic themes (*A rhythm 1* and *A rhythm 2*) using the mute and play tools in the same way that they did for the melodic themes earlier this lesson, using *Composing an A section using a midi sequencer* (printout 12) to help them.

- When pupils have familiarised themselves with each theme, consider as a class:
  - the mood each rhythmic theme creates;
  - how these moods are similar or different to those created by the melodic and accompaniment themes.

TEACHING TIP
Remind pupils that they should restrict themselves to the themes prefixed with an A. They will use the themes prefixed with a B later in the unit.

◀◀ RETURN TO ACTIVITY 4 (page 21)

ICT
(see page 21)

4 **Pupils learn about looping**

10 mins [8] [MIDI]

- Before starting this activity, load the file *ternary.mid* into the sequencer and make sure that it can be heard clearly over the computer's sound system (see *Using a midi sequencer* in the Teacher information section of the CD-ROM for more information).

- Set the left marker to bar 1 and the right marker to the end of bar 11. Make sure loop play is activated and set the sequencer to play. When the pupils have listened to several repetitions of the passage, ask them what they have noticed:

  - the sequencer is repeating the A section;
  - the song position pointer shows where you are in the music;
  - all the tracks are comprised of short repeating themes.

- Explain the term **looping** and that looping is a simple way to extend and emphasise a short theme.

- Explain that looping is:

  - often used in popular music because it is a useful way of creating a strong rhythmic feel which is easy to dance to;
  - also used in classical music by contemporary composers such as Philip Glass and Steve Reich.

- Show pupils how to use the loop function on the sequencer (see *A typical midi sequencer*, printout 8, for more information) and encourage them to experiment with looping different passages from *ternary.mid*.

EXTENSION ACTIVITY

Discuss with pupils the advantages of looping a musical theme live compared to looping it electronically using a sequencer (eg it can be difficult to maintain a steady tempo when looping a theme live, but playing live enables the performer to give more expression to their performance. Electronic looping is quick and simple and makes it easy for composers to create long pieces of music at the touch of a button, but the expression associated with live performance can be lost).

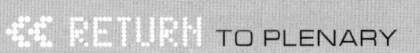

◄◄ RETURN TO PLENARY
(page 22)

Lesson 3

Composing an A section

OBJECTIVES

By the end of the lesson pupils should:

■ understand how theme, timbre and texture can enhance the mood of a composition;

■ be able to combine and loop a melodic and rhythmic theme.

OUTCOMES

Pupils:

☐ compose an A section for their ternary form composition;

☐ perform their A section to the class.

RESOURCES

AUDIO CD
Tracks 4–7, 9–12

CD-ROM
• Presentation
• Video clip 4
• Printouts 2–3, 8–12,14–17
• Midi file (optional)
• Teacher information (optional)

INSTRUMENTS
• Tuned and untuned instruments (optional)
• Electronic keyboards (optional)
• Pupils bring in instruments from home (optional)

ICT
• Whiteboard or computer with data projector and sound
• Midi sequencer software (optional)

Printout 2: Learning intentions lessons 1–6

Focus		
5 mins	2	**Presentation**

■ Display the learning intentions for this lesson using the presentation on the CD-ROM or printout 2.

■ Revise the term **looping** and explain that pupils will now begin to create an A section for their ternary form composition by looping and combining one rhythmic theme and one melodic theme from *Ideas bank A*, which they were introduced to last lesson.

1	**Pupils choose a rhythmic theme for their A section**

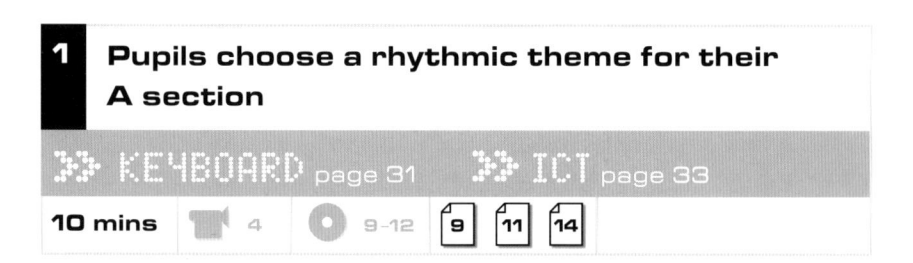

■ Divide the class into groups of four to six pupils and distribute copies of *Composition notepad* (printout 14).

■ Explain that pupils will now begin to create their A section and that they should:

• first, revise each rhythmic theme from *Ideas bank A*;

• decide on the mood they will create in their A section and select a rhythmic theme, which contributes to this mood, to use in their composition;

• consider whether they will perform this rhythmic theme using traditional percussion or beatboxing;

• think about the volume at which they will play this theme and how this could emphasise the mood they are trying to create;

• make a note of the theme, mood, dynamics and timbre they have chosen on printout 14;

• practise looping their rhythmic theme until they can all play it confidently.

TEACHING TIPS

Circulate round the class as they work and help them practise in time to a steady pulse.

Pupils might find it useful to revise the rhythmic themes before they begin, using tracks 9–12 (*Ideas bank A – rhythmic themes 1–4*) or video clip 4 (*Ideas bank A – beatboxed*).

If a drum kit is not available, you will need to help pupils find alternative percussion instruments with which to play the rhythmic themes.

Ensure pupils have their copies of *Ideas bank A* (printout 9) and *Beatboxing* (printout 11) to hand as they work.

2 Pupils add a melodic theme to their A section

KEYBOARD page 32   **ICT** page 34

10 mins   4-7   9   14

- Explain that pupils will now choose a melodic theme for their A section.

- Whilst one pupil loops the chosen rhythmic theme, other pupils in the group experiment with looping each melodic theme from *Ideas bank A* over the top, using any tuned instruments they have available.

- Pupils then:
  - decide which theme best fits the mood they are trying to create in their A section and select a timbre and volume level which reflects this mood;
  - decide whether they will play the melodic theme on just one instrument or use several different timbres;
  - practise looping their melodic theme until they can play it confidently;
  - make a note of the theme, timbre(s) and mood they have chosen on printout 14.

TEACHING TIPS

Ensure pupils have their copies of *Ideas bank A* (printout 9) and *Composition notepad* (printout 14) to hand as they work.

The melodic themes on printout 9 are notated at concert pitch and will need to be transposed for some instruments.

Pupils might find it helpful to revise the melodic themes before they begin, using tracks 4–7 (*Ideas bank A – melodic themes 1–4*).

Circulate round the class as they work and help pupils practise in time to a steady pulse.

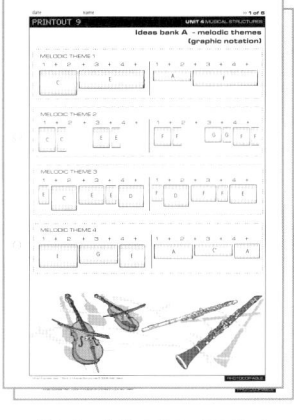

Printout 9: Ideas bank A
(6 pages)

3 Pupils complete their A section

KEYBOARD page 32   **ICT** page 35

10 mins   9   14

- Pupils make sure they have noted down the themes, timbres and mood they have chosen on *Composition notepad* (printout 14).

- They then experiment with playing their chosen rhythmic and melodic themes together and decide whether each theme will start at the same time or will drop in and out of the texture, making a note of their decisions on printout 14 as they work.

- Each group practises their A section until they can play it confidently. They will need to decide:
  - who will play each theme;
  - whether one member of their group needs to direct the performance.

EXTENSION ACTIVITY

Pupils experiment with altering the tempo of their A section and decide which tempo best enhances the mood they are trying to create.

TEACHING TIP

Ensure pupils have their copies of *Ideas bank A* (printout 9) to hand as they work.

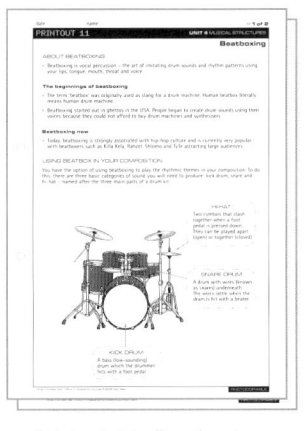

Printout 11: Beatboxing
(2 pages)

Printout 14: Composition
notepad (7 pages)

ASSESSMENT FOR LEARNING

- Do the themes pupils have chosen work well together?

- Who can explain their ideas and contributes well to their group's work?

- Which groups need additional support?

- Who has a clear perception of how timbres, textures and dynamics can influence the mood of a musical theme?

4 **Pupils perform their A section to the class**

10 mins 14

- Invite as many groups as possible to perform their A section to the class.

- Before they perform, each group should use the notes they made on *Composition notepad* (printout 14) to explain to the rest of the class:

  • what mood they have tried to create in their A section;

  • how the themes, timbres and textures they have chosen help create this mood.

- After each performance, discuss as a class whether pupils were successful in creating their intended mood and if not, what could have been improved.

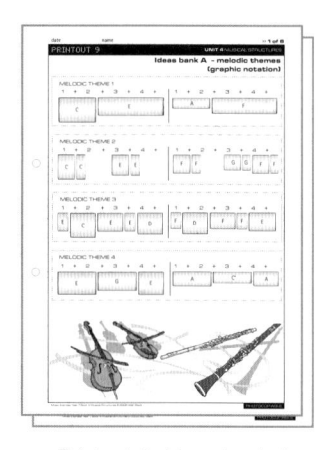

Printout 9: Ideas bank A
(6 pages)

Plenary

5 mins

- Discuss what pupils found most challenging about composing an A section *(eg it might be hard to loop the themes at a steady tempo; their choice of timbres might be limited, depending on the resources available; it could be difficult to combine and perform two themes at once etc).*

Homework 3 17

- Pupils take home *Musical contrasts* (printout 3) and *Key words* (printout 17) to revise for homework.

Printout 3: Musical contrasts
(2 pages)

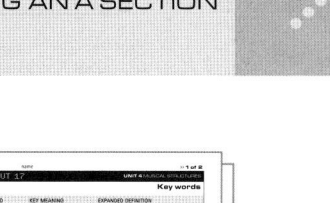

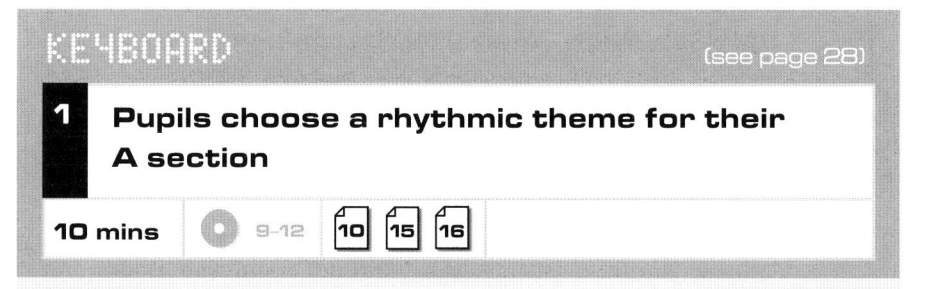

KEYBOARD (see page 28)

1 **Pupils choose a rhythmic theme for their A section**

10 mins ◉ 9–12 [10] [15] [16]

■ Distribute copies of *Composition notepad – keyboard* (printout 15) and *Keyboard effects* (printout 16). Explain that pupils will now begin to create an A section and that they should:

- revise each rhythmic theme from *Ideas bank A*, using the drum kit voice;
- decide on the mood they will create in their A section and select a rhythmic theme, which contributes to this mood, to use in their composition;
- think about the volume at which they will play this theme, and how this could emphasise the mood they are trying to create;
- consider whether they could use any keyboard effects to enhance the mood of the theme they have selected, referring to printout 16 to help them;
- make a note of the theme, mood and any keyboard effects they have chosen on printout 15;
- practise their theme and record six loops of it into the keyboard memory, if keyboards allow.

TEACHING TIPS

Pupils might find it useful to revise the rhythmic themes using tracks 9–12 (*Ideas bank A – rhythmic themes 1–4*).

If keyboards do not have the facility to record, pupils will need to work in pairs or small groups so that there is more than one keyboard between them. One keyboard should be used for the rhythmic themes and the other for the melodic themes.

Ensure pupils have their copies of *Ideas bank A – keyboard* (printout 10) to hand as they work.

◄◄ RETURN TO ACTIVITY 2 (page 29)

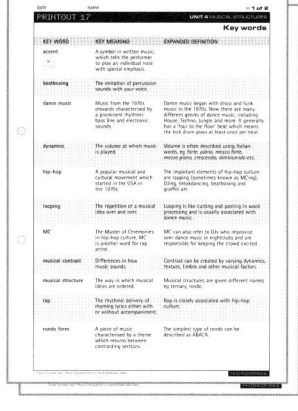
Printout 17: Key words (2 pages)

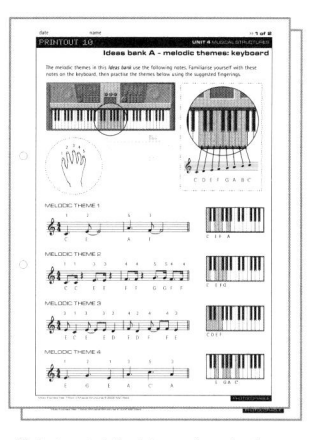
Printout 10: Ideas bank A – keyboard (2 pages)

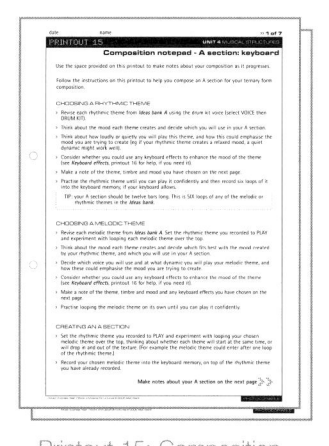
Printout 15: Composition notepad – keyboard (7 pages)

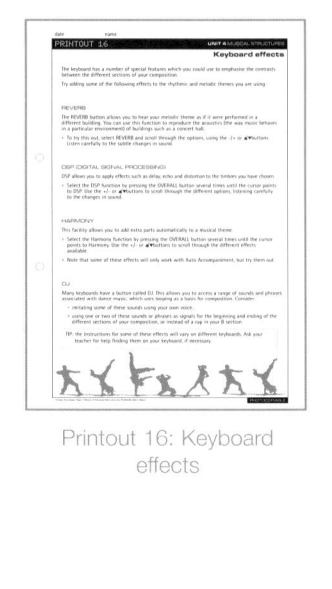

Printout 16: Keyboard effects

KEYBOARD   (see page 29)

2 **Pupils add a melodic theme to their A section**

10 mins   ◉ 4–7   [10] [15] [16]

- Introduce the task as described on page 29 and explain that pupils should:
  - set the rhythmic theme that they recorded into the keyboard memory to play and experiment with looping each melodic theme from *Ideas bank A* over the top;
  - decide which theme best fits the mood they are trying to create in their A section and select a timbre and volume level which reflect this mood;
  - consider whether they could use any keyboard effects to enhance the mood of the theme they have selected, referring to *Keyboard effects* (printout 16) to help them;
  - make a note of the theme, timbres, dynamics and any keyboard effects they have chosen on *Composition notepad – keyboard* (printout 15).

TEACHING TIPS
Pupils might find it helpful to revise the melodic themes using tracks 4–7 (*Ideas bank A – melodic themes 1–4*).

Ensure pupils have their copies of *Ideas bank A – keyboard* (printout 10), *Composition notepad – keyboard* (printout 15) and *Keyboard effects* (printout 16) to hand as they work.

≪ RETURN TO ACTIVITY 3   (page 29)

KEYBOARD   (see page 29)

3 **Pupils complete their A section**

10 mins   [10] [15] [16]

- Pupils make sure they have noted down the themes, timbres, mood and any keyboard effects they have chosen for their A section on *Composition notepad – keyboard* (printout 15), if they have not already done so.

- They set their rhythmic theme to play and experiment with looping their chosen melodic theme over the top, deciding whether it will start at the same time as their rhythmic theme, or will drop in and out of the texture.

- Pupils record their melodic theme into the keyboard memory on top of the rhythmic theme they have already recorded.

TEACHING TIP
Ensure pupils have their copies of *Ideas bank A – keyboard* (printout 10), *Composition notepad – keyboard* (printout 15) and *Keyboard effects* (printout 16) to hand as they work.

EXTENSION ACTIVITY
Show pupils how to alter the tempo on a keyboard. Pupils then experiment with altering the tempo of their A section and decide which tempo best enhances the mood they have created.

≪ RETURN TO ACTIVITY 4   (page 30)

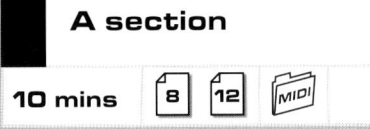

ICT   (see page 28)

1 **Pupils choose a rhythmic theme for their A section**

10 mins   [8] [12] [MIDI]

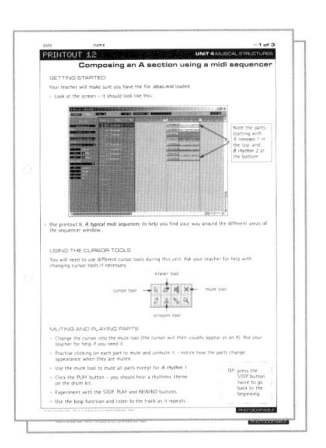

Printout 8: A typical midi sequencer

- Before starting this activity, load the file *ideas.mid* into the sequencer and make sure that it can be heard clearly over the computer's sound system (see *Using a midi sequencer* in the Teacher information section of the CD-ROM for more information). Check that all the parts are muted.

- Make sure pupils have copies of *A typical midi sequencer* (printout 8) and *Composing an A section using a midi sequencer* (printout 12) to hand.

- Explain that pupils will now begin to create an A section for their ternary form composition and will start by choosing a rhythmic theme to use from *ideas.mid*.

- Pupils briefly revise the rhythmic themes, which they were introduced to last lesson, listening to *A rhythm 1* and *A rhythm 2* in turn.

- They decide which rhythmic theme they will use in their A section and select, copy and paste it into a new arrange window starting at bar 1.

- Pupils save their file with a new file name.

Printout 12: Composing an A section using a midi sequencer (3 pages)

TEACHING TIPS

To avoid confusion, it is recommended that the track names found in the left hand column of the arrange window are changed to:

- piano accomp.
- melody
- rhythm

The part names should remain the same.

When pupils save their work, it will be helpful if they use a file format that allows both the *ideas.mid* and composition windows to be saved together in one file (sometimes called a project or song file).

For more information about copying and pasting, see *Using a midi sequencer* in the Teacher information section of the CD-ROM.

You might need to help pupils to open a new arrange window in which to create their A section.

◄◄ RETURN TO ACTIVITY 2   (page 29)

ICT

(see page 29)

2 Pupils add a melodic theme to their A section

10 mins [8] [12] [MIDI]

- Remind pupils that last lesson they listened to each melodic and accompanying theme from *ideas.mid* on its own and thought about the mood that each theme creates.

- Explain that pupils should now listen to how well the melodic and accompanying themes combine, by using the mute and play tools to unmute two themes and listening to them together (for example, *A accomp. 1* and *A melody 1*).

- Pupils decide which two themes contribute best to the mood they are trying to create in their A section.

- They select, copy and paste their chosen themes into their A section, starting at bar 1.

- Pupils then select the three themes they have pasted into their A section and repeat them twice more, following the instructions on *Composing an A section using a midi sequencer* (printout 12).

TEACHING TIPS

For more information about copying and pasting, see *Using a midi sequencer* in the Teacher information section of the CD-ROM.

Ensure pupils have copies of *A typical midi sequencer* (printout 8) and *Composing an A section using a midi sequencer* (printout 12) to hand as they work.

RETURN TO ACTIVITY 3   (page 29)

ICT (see page 29)

3 Pupils complete their A section

10 mins 8 12 MIDI

- Pupils open their composition in the arrange window and consider whether each theme will play constantly or whether they could enhance the mood of their A section by:
  - using the cut and paste tools to allow themes to drop in and out of the texture;
  - altering the patch number(s) of the accompaniment or melody track(s);
  - copying and pasting all or part of one track to a new track with a different patch number, to create a thicker texture.

- Encourage pupils to listen back to their A section at regular intervals to assess how effectively their intended mood is being conveyed.

- Remind pupils to save their work.

EXTENSION ACTIVITY

Demonstrate how to change the tempo of a piece of music in the sequencer. Pupils then experiment with altering the tempo of their A section and decide which tempo best enhances the mood they have created.

TEACHING TIPS

Ensure pupils have copies of *A typical midi sequencer* (printout 8) and *Composing an A section using a midi sequencer* (printout 12) to hand as they work.

Consult your sequencer manual for more information on changing the tempo of a track.

◄◄ RETURN TO ACTIVITY 4 (page 30)

Lesson 4

Composing a B section

OBJECTIVES

By the end of the lesson pupils should:

■ know how to create contrast in a ternary form composition.

OUTCOMES

Pupils:

☐ learn about rap;

☐ create a contrasting B section for their ternary form composition.

RESOURCES

AUDIO CD
Tracks 19–23

CD-ROM
• Presentation
• Video clips 1–3, 5–6
• Printouts 2–3, 8, 14–16, 18–21
• Midi file (optional)
• Teacher information (optional)

INSTRUMENTS
• Tuned and untuned instruments (optional)
• Electronic keyboards (optional)
• Pupils bring in instruments from home (optional)

ICT
• Whiteboard or computer with data projector and sound
• Midi sequencer software (optional)
• Recording equipment (optional)

Focus					
5 mins	● 19	2	3	**Presentation**	

■ Explain the learning intentions for this lesson using the presentation on the CD-ROM or printout 2.

■ Play track 19 (an extract from ***Un granito de arena*** by Ibrahim Ferrer) explaining that this is a piece of Cuban music in ternary form. Using ***Musical contrasts*** (printout 3), discuss how different forms of musical contrast are used in the piece *(eg the A section contrasts in texture, timbre and dynamics to the B section: trumpets dominate the texture and the music is loud but flowing. In the B section, the music relaxes a little and saxophones play a different musical theme, which uses short notes and sounds cheeky)*.

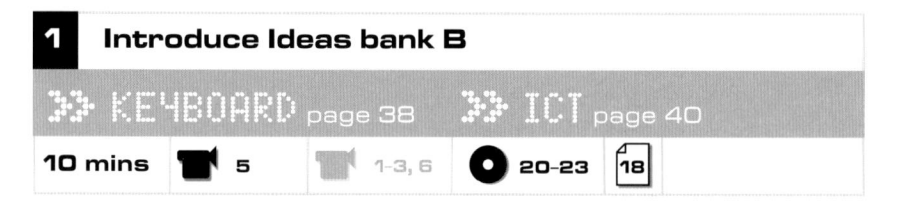

1	**Introduce Ideas bank B**

❯❯ **KEYBOARD** page 38	❯❯ **ICT** page 40
10 mins 📹 5	📹 1–3, 6 ● 20–23 18

■ Display ***Ideas bank B*** (printout 18). Explain that pupils will now create a B section for their ternary form composition and that their B section should:

• contrast in mood with their A section;

• combine one rhythmic theme from ***Ideas bank B*** and a rap.

■ Play tracks 20–23 (***Ideas bank B – rhythmic themes 1–4***) and listen to how the rhythmic themes sound when played on a drum kit. Encourage pupils to follow the notation on printout 18 as they listen.

■ Play video clip 5 (***Ideas bank B – beatboxed***) to show pupils how the rhythmic themes could be beatboxed, encouraging them to follow the beatbox notation on printout 18 as they listen. After each theme, pause the video clip and:

• revise as a class the individual sounds which are used in the theme;

• then, beatbox each theme slowly together.

TEACHING TIPS

You may find it useful to use video clips 1–3 (***Kick drum, snare drum and hi-hat sounds – beatboxed***) when revising the beatboxed sounds used in each rhythmic theme.

You might like to show video clip 6 (***Beatboxing skills showcase – performed by TyTe***) to remind pupils of the variety of sounds which can be produced when beatboxing.

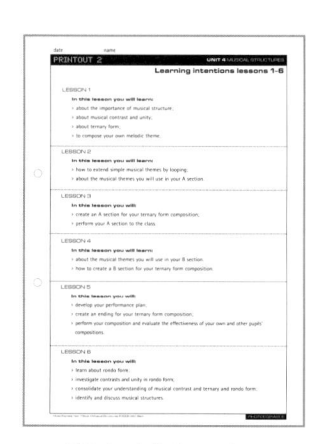

Printout 2: Learning intentions lessons 1–6

2 Pupils choose a theme from Ideas bank B

KEYBOARD page 39   **ICT** page 41

10 mins [14] [18]

- Ensure pupils have copies of *Composition notepad* (printout 14) and *Ideas bank B* (printout 18) to hand and explain that pupils should:
  - first, revise each rhythmic theme from *Ideas bank B*;
  - decide what mood they will create in their B section and select one rhythmic theme, which contributes to this mood, to use in their composition;
  - consider whether they will perform their chosen rhythmic theme using traditional percussion or beatboxing;
  - think about the volume at which they will play this theme and how this could emphasise the mood they are trying to create;
  - make a note of the theme, mood and timbre they have chosen on printout 14;
  - practise looping their rhythmic theme until they can all play it confidently.

3 Introduce rap

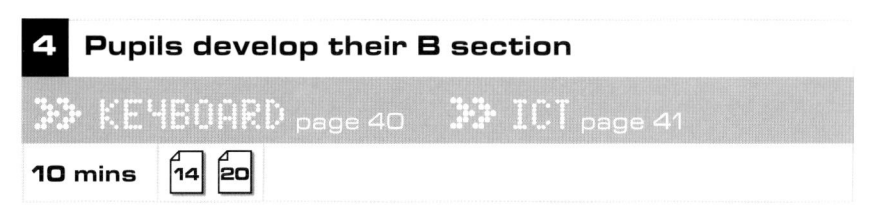

KEYBOARD page 39

10 mins [20]

- Distribute copies of *Rapping* (printout 20) and ask pupils if they already know anything about rap.

- Define the terms **rap, hip-hop** and **MC** and tell pupils that rap could be a good way to create a contrasting B section for their composition.

- Slowly read through the rap on printout 20 as a class, then tap a steady pulse and ask the class to perform the rap together.

- Ask pupils how they think a rap could reflect different moods *(eg the words of the rap could be happy or sad; the speed at which the words are spoken could be fast and create an exciting mood, or slow and create a relaxed mood).*

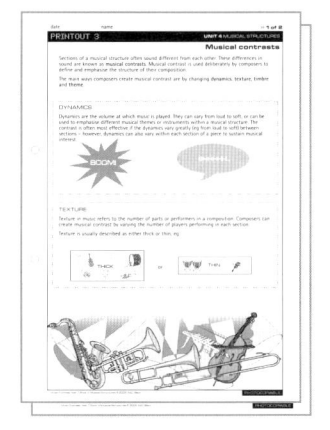

Printout 3: Musical contrasts (2 pages)

4 Pupils develop their B section

KEYBOARD page 40   **ICT** page 41

10 mins [14] [20]

- Pupils use this time to add a rap to their B section. Explain that they should:
  - decide whether they will use the words on *Rapping* (printout 20) or invent their own and how this rap will reflect the mood they are trying to create in their B section;
  - think about whether the rap will be continuous or will drop in and out of the texture;
  - write down the words of their rap on printout 20 and any other decisions they make on *Composition notepad* (printout 14).

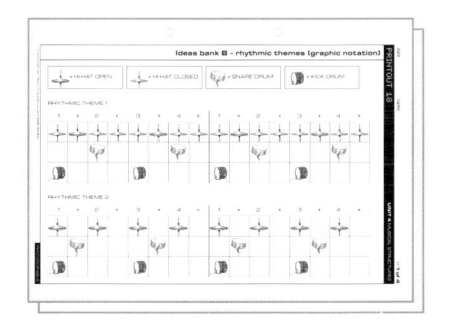

Printout 18: Ideas bank B (4 pages)

ASSESSMENT FOR LEARNING

- Which groups are performing their theme rhythmically?

- Who recognises how a rap can create different moods?

- Who has a clear perception of how timbres, textures and dynamics can be used to create contrasting moods?

Printout 14: Composition notepad (7 pages)

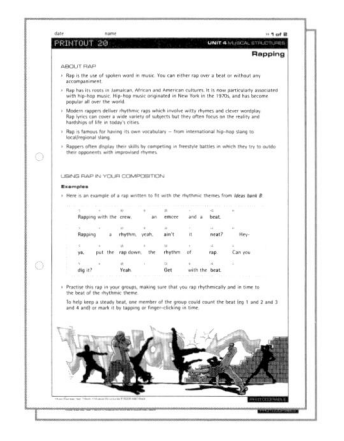

Printout 20: Rapping (2 pages)

- One pupil then loops the chosen rhythmic theme, whilst other pupils take it in turns to practise their rap over the top.

EXTENSION ACTIVITY
Pupils begin to practise the join between their A and B sections, making sure the rapper knows when to come in.

TEACHING TIP
Circulate round the class as they work and help pupils practise in time to a steady pulse.

Plenary 5 mins [14]

- Draw pupils' attention to the performance plan on *Composition notepad* (printout 14) and discuss how a diagram like this could help pupils structure their own composition, eg:

  - it is a useful record of ideas to remember for next lesson;
  - it shows how the piece evolves and the shaded areas show where each theme begins and ends and how many times it is looped;
  - it shows changes in dynamics.

Homework [14]

- Pupils use the blank performance plan and the notes they made on *Composition notepad* (printout 14) to notate the A and B sections they have composed so far, following the guidance on the printout.

KEYBOARD (see page 36)

1 Introduce Ideas bank B

10 mins ● 20-23 [19]

- Display the rhythmic themes on *Ideas bank B – keyboard* (printout 19) and explain the rhythmic notation using the percussion key on the printout.

- Remind pupils how to select the drum kit voice and revise as a class which keys make the kick drum, snare drum and hi-hat sounds.

- Demonstrate the rhythmic themes on printout 19 yourself, or use tracks 20–23 (*Ideas bank B – rhythmic themes 1–4*), and suggest suitable fingerings.

- Pupils then familiarise themselves with the themes using their keyboards.

TEACHING TIP
If you prefer, you could teach the pupils the rhythmic themes aurally, before introducing rhythmic notation.

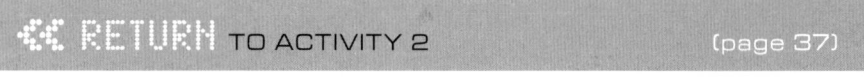

RETURN TO ACTIVITY 2 (page 37)

KEYBOARD (see page 37)

2 | Pupils choose a theme from Ideas bank B

10 mins `15` `16` `19`

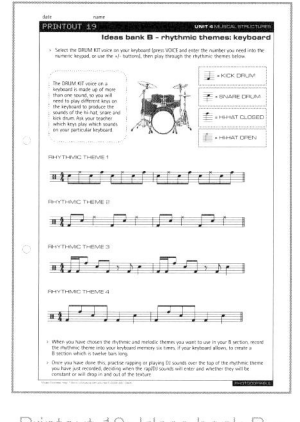

Printout 19: Ideas bank B – keyboard

- Ensure pupils have their copies of *Composition notepad – keyboard* (printout 15) to hand and introduce the task, as described on page 37.

- Explain that pupils should:

  - decide on the mood they will create in their B section and select one rhythmic theme, which contributes to this mood, to use in their composition;

  - think about the volume at which they will play this theme, and how this could emphasise the mood they are trying to create;

  - consider whether they could use any keyboard effects to enhance the mood of the theme, using *Keyboard effects* (printout 16) to help them;

  - make a note of the theme, mood, dynamics and any effects they have chosen on printout 15;

  - practise their theme and record six loops of it into the keyboard memory, if keyboards allow, following the instructions on printout 15.

TEACHING TIPS

Circulate round the class as they work and help them practise in time to a steady pulse.
Ensure pupils have their copies of *Ideas bank B – keyboard* (printout 19) to hand as they work.

RETURN TO ACTIVITY 3 (page 37)

Printout 15: Composition notepad – keyboard (7 pages)

KEYBOARD (see page 37)

3 | Introduce rap

10 mins `16` `20`

- Distribute copies of *Rapping* (printout 20) and ask pupils if they know anything about rap already.

- Define the terms **rap, hip-hop** and **MC** and tell pupils that rap could be a good way to create a contrasting B section for their composition.

- Ask pupils how they think a rap could reflect different moods *(eg the words of the rap could be happy or sad; the speed at which the words are spoken could be fast and create an exciting mood, or slow and create a relaxed mood).*

- Using *Keyboard effects* (printout 16), introduce the DJ function to the pupils, if your keyboard has one. Explain that in their B section, pupils could either use the rap on printout 20, invent their own words, or use the DJ function on their keyboard to create a rap-like rhythmic section using sampled vocal sounds.

- Tap a steady pulse and encourage different pupils to improvise short rhythmic passages using DJ sounds, if their keyboards allow.

TEACHING TIP

If keyboards do not have a DJ function, ask pupils to perform the rap on printout 20 while you tap a steady pulse.

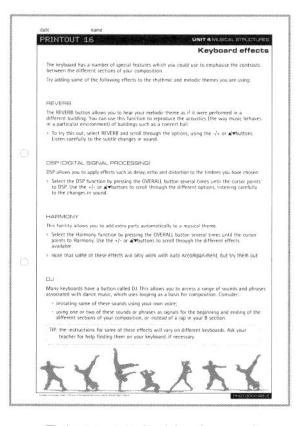

Printout 16: Keyboard effects

RETURN TO ACTIVITY 4 (page 37)

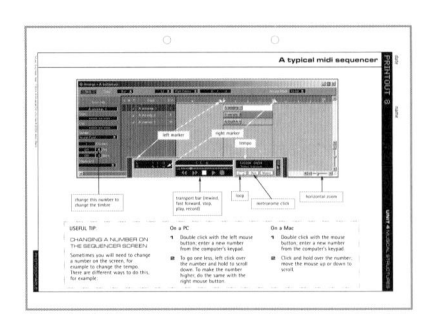

Printout 8: A typical midi sequencer

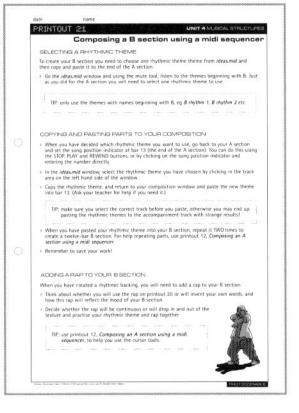

Printout 21: Composing a B section using a midi sequencer

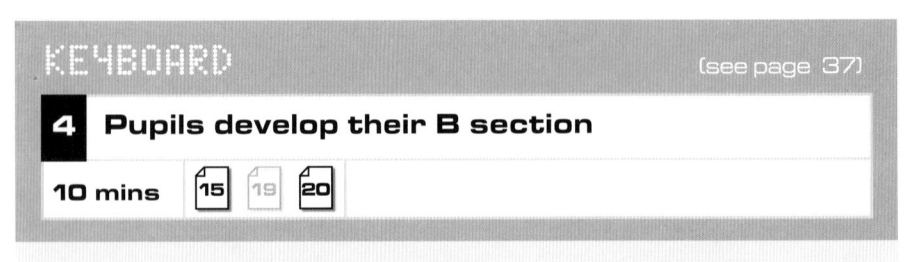

KEYBOARD (see page 37)

4 Pupils develop their B section

10 mins | 15 | 19 | 20 |

- Pupils use this time to add a rap to their B section. Explain that they should:
  - decide whether they will use the words on *Rapping* (printout 20), invent their own, or create a rap-like rhythmic section using DJ sounds, and how this will reflect the mood they are trying to create in their B section;
  - think about whether the rap/DJ sounds will be continuous or will drop in and out of the texture;
  - make a note of their rap/DJ sounds on printout 20 and any other decisions they make on *Composition notepad – keyboard* (printout 15);
  - set the rhythmic theme that they recorded into the keyboard memory to play and practise rapping or playing DJ sounds over the top.

EXTENSION ACTIVITY

Pupils begin to practise the join between their A and B sections, making sure the rapper knows when to come in.

TEACHING TIPS

Pupils using DJ sounds could record them into the keyboard memory, if keyboards allow. Pupils might find it useful to have copies of *Ideas bank B – keyboard* (printout 19) to hand as they work.

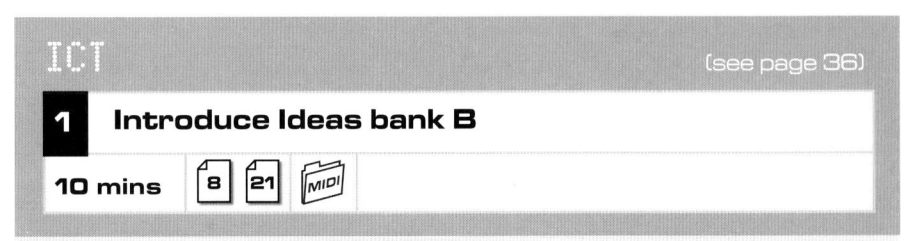

RETURN TO PLENARY (page 38)

ICT (see page 36)

1 Introduce Ideas bank B

10 mins | 8 | 21 | MIDI |

- Before starting this activity, load the file *ideas.mid* into the midi sequencer and make sure that it can be heard clearly over the computer's sound system (see *Using a midi sequencer* in the Teacher information section of the CD-ROM for more information). Check that all the parts are muted.

- Distribute copies of *Composing a B section using a midi sequencer* (printout 21) and introduce the task, as described on page 36.

- Pupils listen to *B rhythm 1* and *B rhythm 2* in turn, using the mute and play tools and following the instructions on printout 21.

- Discuss as a class the mood each rhythmic theme creates *(eg B rhythm 1 creates a funky mood because the rhythm is unpredictable. B rhythm 2 has a constant beat on the kick drum which makes it sound bold).*

TEACHING TIP

Ensure pupils have copies of *A typical midi sequencer* (printout 8) to hand as they work.

RETURN TO ACTIVITY 2 (page 37)

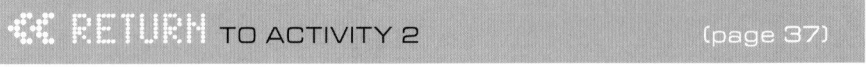

ICT   (see page 37)

2   Pupils choose a theme from Ideas bank B

10 mins   8   21   MIDI

- Pupils:

  - consider which rhythmic theme contrasts most effectively with that of their A section, listening again to each theme if necessary;
  - decide which theme they will use in their composition and select, copy and paste this theme into their composition, starting at bar 13;
  - select the theme they have just pasted and repeat it twice more to create a rhythmic backing for their B section.

- Remind pupils to save their work.

TEACHING TIPS

The length of the B section can be changed later, if desired, to accommodate a longer rap. For more information about copying and pasting, see *Using a midi sequencer* in the Teacher information section of the CD-ROM.

Ensure pupils have copies of *A typical midi sequencer* (printout 8) and *Composing a B section using a midi sequencer* (printout 21) to hand as they work.

RETURN TO ACTIVITY 3   (page 37)

ICT   (see page 37)

4   Pupils develop their B section

10 mins   8   20   21   MIDI

- Pupils use this time to add a rap to their B section. Explain that they should:

  - decide whether they will use the words on *Rapping* (printout 20) or invent their own and how this rap will reflect the mood they are trying to create in their B section;
  - think about whether the rap will be continuous or will drop in and out of the texture;
  - write down the words of their rap on printout 20, if necessary.

- Pupils set their B section to play and practise rapping over the top.

EXTENSION ACTIVITY

Pupils begin to practise the join between their A and B sections, making sure the rapper knows when to come in.

TEACHING TIPS

Ensure pupils have copies of *A typical midi sequencer* (printout 8) and *Composing a B section using a midi sequencer* (printout 21) to hand as they work.

If your sequencer allows, pupils could record their rap live on to a new track. Consult your sequencer manual for more information on recording live instruments.

RETURN TO PLENARY   (page 38)

Lesson 5 — Developing and performing

OBJECTIVES

By the end of the lesson pupils should:

- be able to create a convincing ending;
- understand the purpose of writing down a musical structure.

OUTCOMES

Pupils:

- ☐ complete their ternary form composition;
- ☐ perform their ternary form composition to the class;
- ☐ assess and evaluate their own and other pupils' compositions.

RESOURCES

CD-ROM

- Presentation
- Printouts 2, 8, 14–15, 20, 22–26
- Midi file (optional)
- Teacher information (optional)

INSTRUMENTS

- Tuned and untuned instruments (optional)
- Electronic keyboards (optional)
- Pupils bring in instruments from home (optional)

ICT

- Whiteboard or computer with data projector and sound
- Midi sequencer software (optional)
- Recording equipment (optional)

Printout 2: Learning intentions lessons 1–6

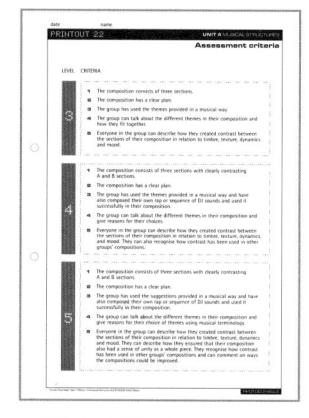

Printout 22: Assessment criteria

Focus

5 mins [2] [22]   **Presentation**

- Explain the learning intentions for this lesson using the presentation on the CD-ROM or printout 2.

- Display *Assessment criteria* (printout 22) and go through it with the class, making sure that pupils understand the level descriptions and the importance of creating a clear sense of contrast and unity between the different sections of their composition.

1 Pupils create their final A section

10 mins [14] [23]

- Distribute copies of *Finishing touches* (printout 23) and remind pupils that:
  - they have now composed an A and B section for a piece in ternary form;
  - a ternary form piece should have three sections, so pupils will need to repeat their A section after their B section to create an ABA structure;
  - repeating the A section at the end of their composition will help to give the structure a sense of unity.

- Explain that when pupils repeat their A section, they do not have to use the same timbres or textures as they used before *(eg if a trumpet performed the melodic theme in the first A section, a clarinet and violin could play it in the second A section)*.

- Encourage groups to try out their ideas and then work together to fill in their final A section on their performance plan, considering:
  - which timbres they will use and whether these will create a different texture to their first A section;
  - whether the dynamics of their final A section will be different to the first.

TEACHING TIPS

Circulate round the class as they work and help them practise in time to a steady pulse. Ensure pupils have their copies of *Composition notepad* (printout 14) to hand as they work.

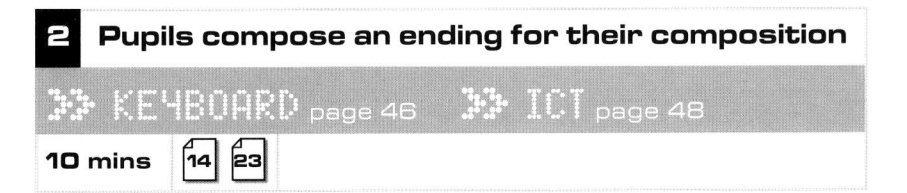

2 Pupils compose an ending for their composition

>> KEYBOARD page 46   **>> ICT** page 48

10 mins [14] [23]

■ Explain that pupils will now create an ending for their composition and could use any of the suggestions on printout 23, or invent their own ending.

■ Demonstrate the suggested ending on printout 23 yourself.

■ Groups explore the ideas for endings given on printout 23. They decide which ending they will use in their composition and make a note of this ending on their performance plan (printout 14).

■ Pupils then practise the join between their final A section and ending.

TEACHING TIPS

The musical theme on printout 23 is notated at concert pitch and will need to be transposed for some instruments.

Ensure pupils have copies of *Composition notepad* (printout 14) and *Finishing touches* (printout 23) to hand as they work.

Circulate round the class as they work and help pupils practise in time to a steady pulse.

3 Pupils practise their composition

>> KEYBOARD page 46   **>> ICT** page 49

10 mins [14] [20]

■ In their groups, pupils practise their composition using the performance plan they have created on printout 14. Encourage them to:

• first, revise each theme separately, then rehearse all the parts together;

• practise the joins between sections to make sure their performance is fluid;

• try to reflect the contrasts between sections as much as possible in their performance.

EXTENSION ACTIVITY

If possible, record or video each composition to help groups assess whether they are enhancing or detracting from the musical contrasts through their playing.

TEACHING TIPS

Ensure pupils have their copies of *Composition notepad* (printout 14) and *Rapping* (printout 20) to hand as they work.

Circulate round the class as they work and help pupils practise in time to a steady pulse.

ASSESSMENT FOR LEARNING

• Who understands how to use musical themes to create contrast?

• Who demonstrates an ability to get the most value from a musical theme?

• Whose composition is musically well-balanced?

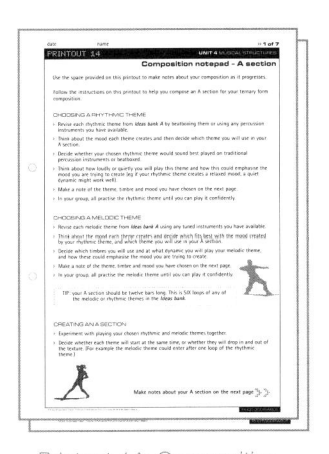

Printout 14: Composition notepad (7 pages)

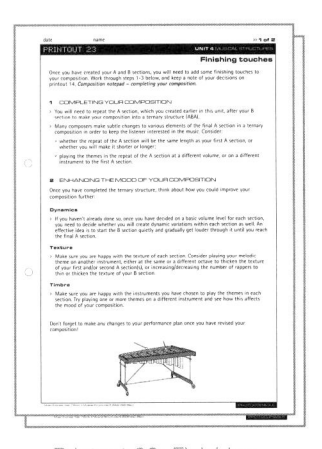

Printout 23: Finishing touches (2 pages)

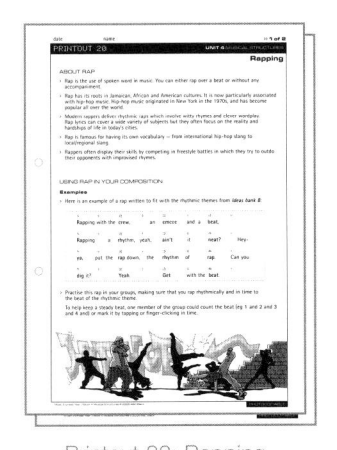

Printout 20: Rapping (2 pages)

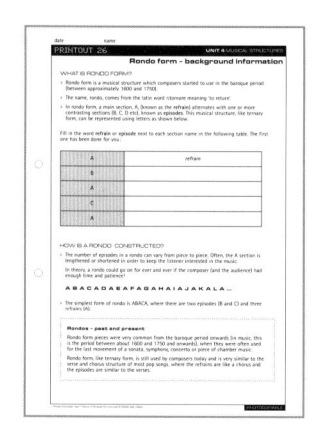

Printout 26: Rondo form –
background information

4 **Pupils perform their composition to the class**

10 mins [14] [20] [22]

■ Pupils perform their composition to the class, using their performance plan (printout 14) and *Rapping* (printout 20). Before presenting their work, each group should explain:

- how they have created contrast and unity between the different sections of their composition, referring specifically to texture, timbre and dynamics;
- anything else they want to mention about the style or mood of their piece.

■ After each group has performed their composition, discuss as a class whether:

- the group chose themes which worked well together and created effective textural, timbral and dynamic contrasts between their A and B sections;
- the intended moods were conveyed effectively;
- there was a sense of unity about their composition, or whether the A and B sections sounded like separate compositions.

TEACHING TIPS

If possible, record each group's composition and play it back to illustrate the discussion.

Pupils might find it useful to have *Assessment criteria* (printout 22) to refer to when they present their work.

Plenary

5 mins [22]

■ Ask pupils to discuss which level they think their own composition reached and why, taking into account the feedback from the class and the level descriptions on *Assessment criteria* (printout 22).

Homework [26]

■ Distribute copies of *Rondo form – background information* (printout 26) and ask pupils to read it for homework.

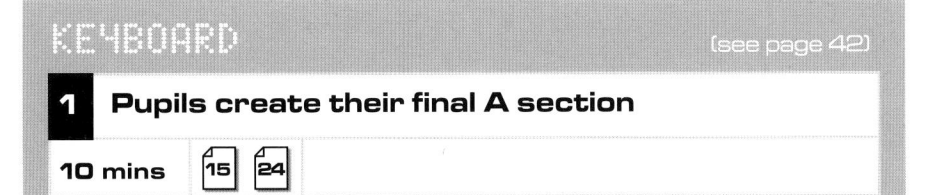

KEYBOARD (see page 42)

1 Pupils create their final A section

10 mins [15] [24]

- Distribute copies of *Finishing touches – keyboard* (printout 24) and remind pupils that:

  • they have now composed an A and B section for a piece in ternary form;
  • a ternary form piece should have three sections, so pupils will need to repeat their A section after their B section to create an ABA structure;
  • repeating the A section at the end of their composition will help to give the structure a sense of unity.

- Explain that when pupils repeat their A section, they don't have to use the same timbres or textures they used before *(eg if they used a trumpet timbre for the melodic theme in the first A section, a clarinet and violin timbre could be used in the second A section).*

- Pupils work at their keyboards to fill in their final A section on their performance plan (printout 15), considering:

  • which timbres they will use and whether these will create a different texture to their first A section;
  • whether the dynamics of their final A section will be different to their first A section.

- Pupils record their final A section into a separate user area of the keyboard memory, if it is different from their first A section.

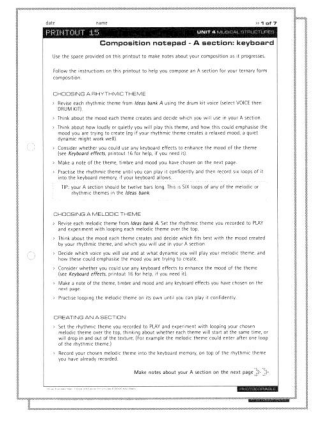

Printout 15: Composition
notepad – keyboard
(7 pages)

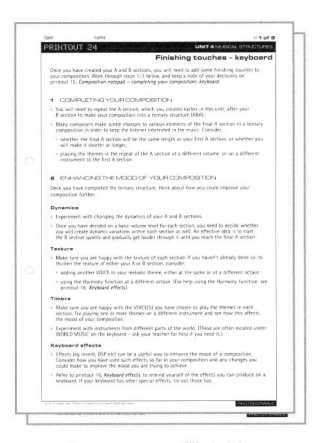

Printout 24: Finishing
touches – keyboard
(2 pages)

TEACHING TIPS

Encourage pupils to try out their ideas before filling in the final A section on their performance plan.

You may need to remind pupils that they will need to record each theme separately when recording their final A section, as they did when creating their first A section.

Encourage pupils to use the metronome function on their keyboard to help them keep a steady tempo.

Ensure pupils have copies of *Composition notepad – keyboard* (printout 15) to hand as they work.

RETURN TO ACTIVITY 2 (page 43)

KEYBOARD   (see page 43)

2 Pupils compose an ending for their composition

10 mins   [15] [24]

- Introduce the task as described on page 43 and demonstrate the ending on printout 24 yourself, suggesting suitable fingerings.

- Pupils explore the different ideas for endings given on printout 24 and decide which ending they will use in their composition, keeping a note of their ending on their performance plan (printout 15).

- Pupils record their chosen ending into the keyboard memory, if necessary, in a separate user area to that in which they recorded their A and B sections. (If pupils choose to fade out, they should set their final A section to play and practise fading out using the volume control.)

TEACHING TIPS

If pupils choose to fade out, they will need to notate this in the dynamics section of their performance plan.

If pupils made changes to their second A section and recorded it into the keyboard memory, they could add their ending onto this, rather than recording it separately.

RETURN TO ACTIVITY 3   (page 43)

KEYBOARD   (see page 43)

3 Pupils practise their composition

10 mins   [15] [20]

- Pupils practise their composition using the performance plan they have created on printout 15. Encourage them to:
  - first, rehearse each section separately, or listen back to each section if they are pre-recorded;
  - practise the joins between sections to make sure their performance is fluid;
  - decide who will be responsible for operating the volume control and/or keyboard effects and who will toggle between user areas;
  - decide who will perform the rap and whether they need to appoint a director to signal when the rapper should begin.

EXTENSION ACTIVITY

If possible, record or video each composition to help pupils assess whether the contrasts they have created between their A and B sections are effective or whether anything needs to be modified.

TEACHING TIP

Ensure pupils have copies of *Composition notepad – keyboard* (printout 15) and *Rapping* (printout 20) to hand as they work.

RETURN TO ACTIVITY 4   (page 44)

ICT

(see page 42)

1 Pupils create their final A section

10 mins `8` `25` `MIDI`

■ Distribute copies of *Finishing touches – ICT* (printout 25) and remind pupils that:

- they have now composed an A and B section for a piece in ternary form;
- a ternary form piece should have three sections, so pupils will need to repeat their A section after their B section to create an ABA structure;
- repeating the A section at the end of their composition will help to give the structure a sense of unity.

■ Explain that pupils should copy and paste their A section so that it repeats after their B section, using printout 25 to help them.

■ Pupils then work on enhancing the mood and contrasts within their composition, making any adjustments to dynamics, balance, texture, timbre and special effects that they feel necessary, as described on printout 25.

■ Encourage pupils to consider:

- whether they are happy with when each theme enters and any special effects they have applied to the themes;
- whether the textures and timbres of each section effectively enhance the intended mood and whether there is sufficient contrast in texture and timbre between their A and B sections.

TEACHING TIPS

For more information on copying and pasting, see *Using a midi sequencer* in the Teacher information section of the CD-ROM.

Pupils might find it useful to have *A typical midi sequencer* (printout 8) to hand as they work.

Consult your sequencer manual for more information on using special effects.

«« RETURN TO ACTIVITY 2 (page 43)

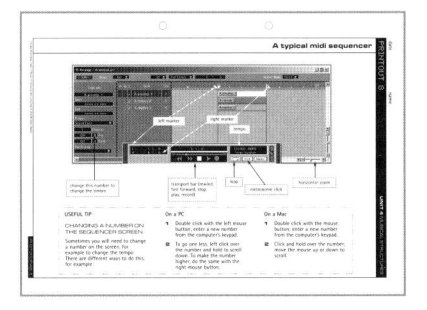

Printout 8: A typical midi sequencer

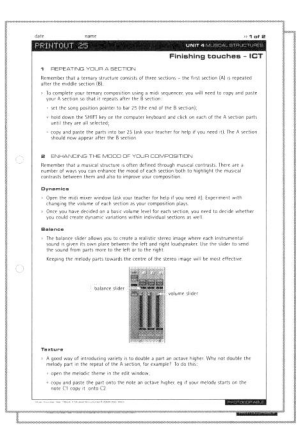

Printout 25: Finishing touches – ICT (2 pages)

ICT   (see page 43)

2 Pupils compose an ending for their composition

10 mins   8   25   MIDI

- Explain that pupils will now create an ending for their composition and that they could use any of the suggestions on *Finishing touches – ICT* (printout 25), or invent their own ending.

- Demonstrate the ending suggested on printout 25 yourself.

- Pupils explore the ideas for endings given on printout 25. They decide which they will use in their composition and make the appropriate adjustments to their file.

- Remind pupils to save their work.

TEACHING TIPS

Ensure pupils have copies of *A typical midi sequencer* (printout 8) to hand as they work.

You might need to consult your sequencer manual to help pupils create a fade out at the end of their composition.

RETURN TO ACTIVITY 3   (page 43)

ICT   (see page 43)

| **3** | **Pupils practise their composition** |

10 mins

■ Pupils practise their composition using the notes they made on *Rapping* (printout 20) to remind them of their rap, if required. Encourage them to:

- first, listen back to their whole composition;
- consider who will be responsible for starting and stopping the sequencer;
- decide who will perform the rap and whether they need to appoint a director to signal when the rapper should begin.

■ Pupils then rehearse their composition until they can perform it confidently.

EXTENSION ACTIVITY

Demonstrate how to open the midi mixer window. (This is usually done from one of the menus at the top of the screen, eg the Panels or Windows menu.) You will see a volume slider for each track. Encourage pupils to enhance the mood of their composition by:

- using the volume sliders to change the volume level of each track whilst playing the composition, so that each part can be heard clearly;
- changing the volume of a track during the course of the piece;
- making adjustments to the left/right balance of each track to create an effective stereo image.

◀◀ RETURN TO ACTIVITY 4   (page 44)

Lesson 6 Rondo form

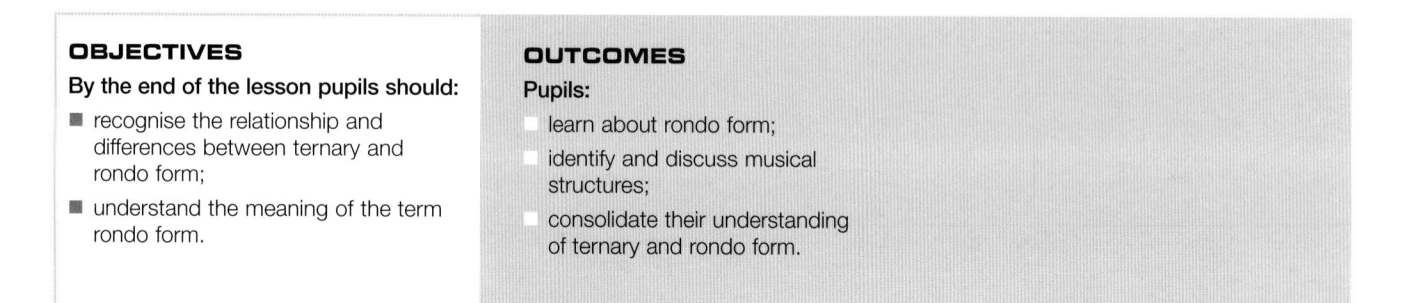

OBJECTIVES

By the end of the lesson pupils should:

- recognise the relationship and differences between ternary and rondo form;
- understand the meaning of the term rondo form.

OUTCOMES

Pupils:

- learn about rondo form;
- identify and discuss musical structures;
- consolidate their understanding of ternary and rondo form.

RESOURCES

AUDIO CD
Tracks 24–26

CD-ROM
- Presentation
- Printouts 1–2, 26–29
- Midi file (optional)
- Teacher information (optional)

ICT
- Whiteboard or computer with data projector and sound
- Midi sequencer software (optional)

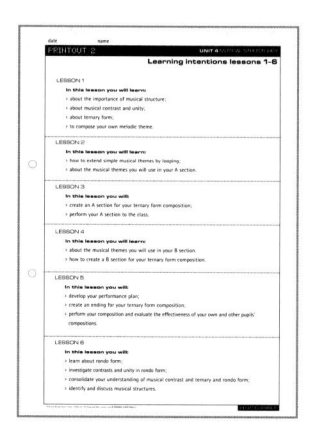

Printout 2: Learning intentions lessons 1–6

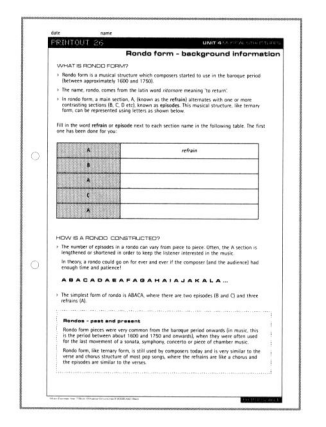

Printout 26: Rondo form – background information

Focus

- Explain the learning intentions for this lesson using the presentation on the CD-ROM or printout 2.

- Define the term **rondo form** and go through *Rondo form – background information* (printout 26), which the pupils read for homework.

1 Introduce rondo form

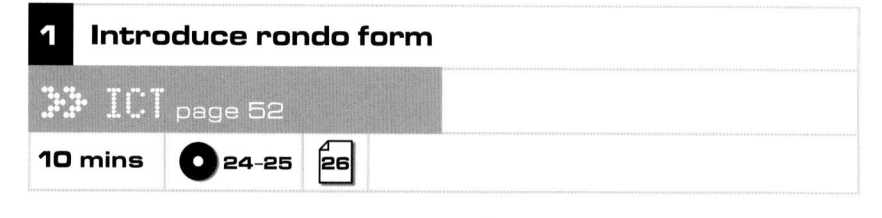

- Listen to *Quadrille – ABA* and *Quadrille – ABACA* (tracks 24 and 25) and consider as a class what they have in common in terms of structure *(tracks 24 and 25 begin in the same way, but track 25 is longer – it has two extra sections)*.

- Play tracks 24 and 25 again and ask pupils to describe the structure of these tracks using letters *(track 24 = ABA, track 25 = ABACA)*.

- Explain that track 25 is in rondo form, which the pupils read about for homework.

- Ask pupils how they would describe the structure of *Quadrille* (track 25) using the terms 'episode' and 'refrain', referring to *Rondo form – background information* (printout 26) to help them *(refrain – episode – refrain – episode – refrain)*.

TEACHING TIP

The sections of *Quadrille* are:

- A = 0.00 – 0.14
- B = 0.15 – 0.27
- A = 0.28 – 0.34
- C = 0.35 – 0.47
- A = 0.48 – 0.53

2 Pupils analyse Quadrille

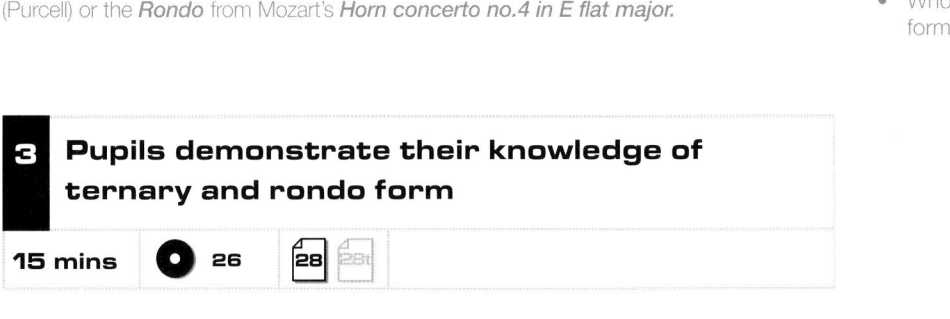

ICT page 53

15 mins ● 25 📄27 📄27t

- Distribute copies of *Quadrille* (printout 27) and go through the questions with the class.

- Play *Quadrille* (track 25) and ask pupils to complete answers to the questions on printout 27 as they listen.

- Go through the answers as a class, replaying the track as necessary.

TEACHING TIPS

Sample answers are provided on *Quadrille – teacher's answer sheet* (printout 27t), if required.

If you would like to offer pupils extra listening for pieces in rondo form, you might like to consider: *Les barricades mystérieuses* (Couperin), *Rondeau* from *Suite from Abdelazar* (Purcell) or the *Rondo* from Mozart's *Horn concerto no.4 in E flat major.*

3 Pupils demonstrate their knowledge of ternary and rondo form

15 mins ● 26 📄28 📄28t

- Distribute copies of *Montagues and Capulets* (printout 28). Introduce the piece and play track 26 several times through.

- Ask pupils to fill in the answers to the questions on printout 28 and go through the answers as a class. Encourage pupils to explain their conclusions and to use the terminology they have learnt in this unit in their responses.

TEACHING TIP

Sample answers are provided on *Montagues and Capulets – teacher's answer sheet* (printout 28t), if required.

Plenary

5 mins 📄1 📄29 **Presentation**

- Remind pupils of the learning intentions for this unit using the presentation on the CD-ROM or printout 1.

- Discuss what the class has enjoyed learning about most in this unit.

- Distribute copies of *End of unit evaluation sheet* (printout 29) and explain how the pupils should complete it for homework.

KEY WORDS

rondo form – a piece of music characterised by a theme which returns between contrasting sections. The simplest type of rondo can be described as ABACA.

ASSESSMENT FOR LEARNING

- When discussing musical contrast do pupils:

  - use the correct musical terminology?

  - make reference to the ideas of contrast they have been taught?

    have a working knowledge of how different timbres, textures and dynamics can be used to create different moods?

- Who can identify ternary and rondo form through aural analysis?

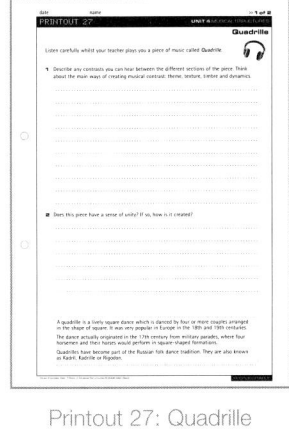

Printout 27: Quadrille

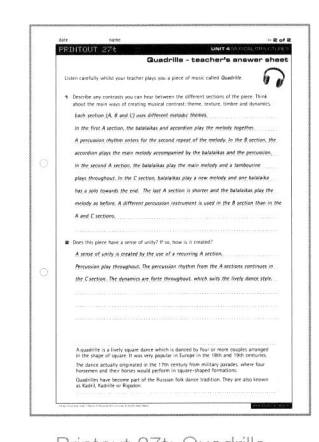

Printout 27t: Quadrille – teacher's answer sheet

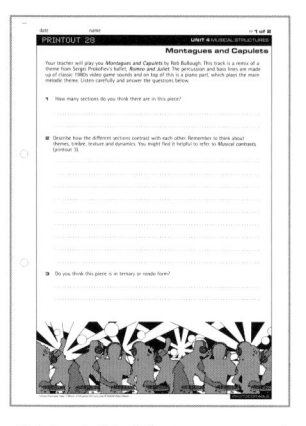

Printout 28: Montagues and Capulets

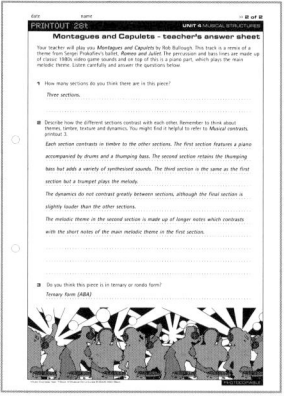

Printout 28t: Montagues and Capulets – teacher's answer sheet

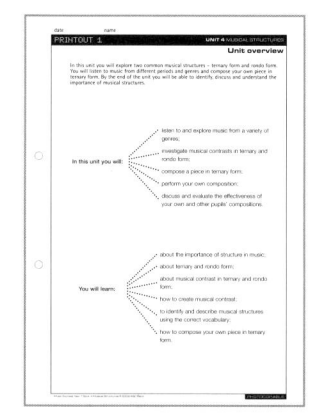

Printout 1: Unit overview

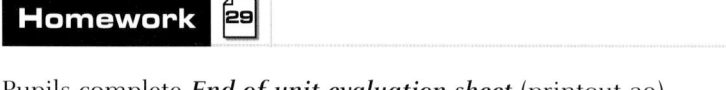

Homework 29

■ Pupils complete *End of unit evaluation sheet* (printout 29).

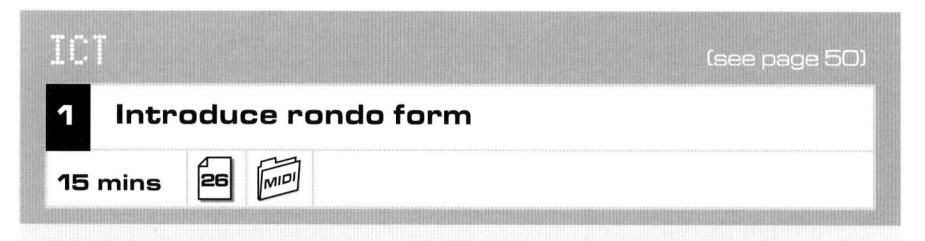

ICT   (see page 50)

1 Introduce rondo form

15 mins 26 MIDI

■ Before starting this activity, make sure the file *quadrille.mid* is loaded into the midi sequencer and that it can be heard clearly over the computer's sound system (see *Using a midi sequencer* in the *Teacher information* section of the CD-ROM for more information).

■ Play *quadrille.mid* and ask pupils what this structure has in common with ternary form *(it begins in the same way, ABA, but there are two extra sections at the end, which create an ABACA structure).*

■ Explain that *quadrille.mid* is in rondo form, which the pupils learnt about for homework.

■ Display the whole song in the arrange window and ask a pupil to point to the area on the display that they think shows the C section. Play the file once more and ask the class to:

· keep their hands lowered during the A sections;

· raise one hand during the B section;

· raise both hands during the C section.

■ Ask pupils how they would describe the structure of *quadrille.mid* using the terms 'episode' and 'refrain', referring to *Rondo form – background information* (printout 26) to help them *(refrain – episode – refrain – episode – refrain).*

TEACHING TIP

The sections of *quadrille.mid* are:

• A = 0.00 – 0.14

• B = 0.15 – 0.27

• A = 0.28 – 0.34

• C = 0.35 – 0.47

• A = 0.48 – 0.54

RETURN TO ACTIVITY 2   (page 51)

ICT   (see page 51)

2 Pupils analyse Quadrille

15 mins [27] [27t] [MIDI]

- Distribute copies of *Quadrille* (printout 27) and go through the questions with the class.

- Play *quadrille.mid* and ask pupils to complete the answers to the questions on printout 27 as they listen.

- Go through the answers as a class, replaying the file as necessary.

TEACHING TIPS

Sample answers are provided on *Quadrille – teacher's answer sheet* (printout 27t), if required.

Play *quadrille.mid* as many times as necessary.

If you would like to offer pupils extra listening for pieces in rondo form, you might like to consider: *Les barricades mystérieuses* (Couperin), *Rondeau* from *Suite from Abdelazar* (Purcell) or the *Rondo* from Mozart's *Horn concerto no.4 in E flat major*.

◄◄ RETURN TO ACTIVITY 3   (page 51)

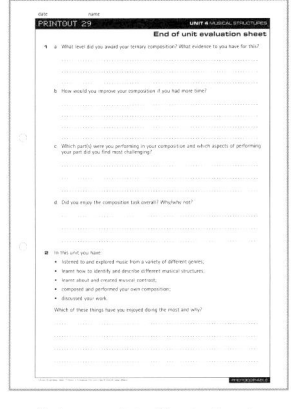

Printout 29: End of unit evaluation sheet

GLOSSARY

accent
A symbol in written music, which tells the performer to play an individual note with special emphasis.

arrange window
The main window on a sequencer that displays the whole song arrangement.

beatboxing
The imitation of percussion sounds with your voice.

dance music
Music from the 1970s onwards, characterised by a prominent rhythmic bass line and electronic sounds. Dance music began with disco and funk music in the 1970s. Now there are many different genres of dance music, including House, Techno, Jungle and more. It generally has a 'four-to-the-floor' beat which means the kick drum plays at least once per beat.

dynamics
The volume at which music is played. Volume is often described using Italian words, eg *forte, piano, mezzo forte, mezzo piano, crescendo, diminuendo* etc.

freeware
Software freely available without charge.

hip-hop
A popular musical and cultural movement which started in the USA in the 1970s. The important elements of hip-hop culture are rapping (sometimes known as MCing), DJing, breakdancing, beatboxing and graffiti art.

left/right marker
A marked point in the sequencer arrange window. This is sometimes called a left/right locator.

looping
The repetition of a musical idea over and over. Looping is like cutting and pasting in word processing and is usually associated with dance music.

MC
The Master of Ceremonies: in hip-hop culture, MC is another word for rap artist. MC can also refer to DJs who improvise over dance music in nightclubs and are responsible for keeping the crowd excited.

midi
Musical Instrument Digital Interface – a language that allows compatible software and hardware to communicate.

midi mixer
A window that allows mute, solo and volume changes for each sequencer track.

musical contrast
Differences in how music sounds. Contrast can be created by varying dynamics, texture, timbre and other musical factors.

musical structure
The way in which musical ideas are ordered. Musical structures are given different names, eg ternary, rondo. Structure can also refer to how a piece of music divides into sections, eg beginning, middle and end.

mute
To silence a sequencer track.

note
A symbol used in staff notation to indicate the pitch and duration of a sound.

pitch	The complete range of sounds in music from the highest to the lowest. A general rule of thumb in music is the larger the instrument, the lower its pitch.
rap	The rhythmic delivery of rhyming lyrics either with or without accompaniment. Rap is closely associated with hip-hop culture.
register	A specific range of a voice or instrument.
rondo form	A piece of music characterised by a theme which returns between contrasting sections. The simplest type of rondo can be described as ABACA.
scale	An arrangement of specific notes played in order of pitch from the lowest to the highest (or vice versa). We choose notes for compositions from scales: scales therefore give character to music.
sequencer	Software for recording, composing and arranging music, which can have midi or audio tracks.
shareware	Software subject to a registration fee.
SMF	Standard Midi File – a basic midi file format that can be recognised by different software packages.
soundcard	A hardware device installed in a computer which creates the sound output. It often includes a midi interface.
step time input	Recording music into a sequencer one note at a time, for example, by using the pen tool.
stereo image	The position of sounds between left and right loudspeakers.
tempo	The speed of the steady beat. Tempo is often described using Italian words, eg *allegro, andante, moderato, presto, vivace* etc.
ternary form	A piece of music in three sections: the first and third sections are similar and the second section is different. Ternary form is also known as ABA form.
texture	The number of parts or performers in a piece. Some pieces are written for a set number of performers and these create particular textures, eg solo, duet, trio, quartet and quintet.
timbre	The unique characteristic sound of each instrument. Every instrument, including the human voice, has its own particular sound.
time signature	A time signature indicates how many beats there are in a bar. For example, $\frac{4}{4}$ means four crotchet beats in a bar.
theme	A musical idea, which is an important element in the structure of a piece of music. Different themes can create different moods.
voice	An individual instrument sound or special effect on a keyboard. Most voices are grouped into categories or families and printed on the keyboard panel.

ACKNOWLEDGEMENTS

The authors and publishers would like to thank the following teachers, consultants and colleagues who assisted in the preparation of this book:

Jamie Acton-Bond, Naomi Barker, Rob Bullough, Stephen Chadwick, Tatiana Demidova, Maureen Hanke, Christopher Hussey, Erika Jenkins, Matthew Jones, Harriet Lowe, Jocelyn Lucas, Susan McIntyre, Karen Manning, Carla Moss, Sophie Nathan, Cath Rasbash, Jeanne Roberts, Sheena Roberts, Ian Shepherd, Rebecca Taylor, Gavin Tyte and Emily Wilson.

The following have kindly granted permission for the inclusion of their copyright materials in *Music Express Year 7 Book 4: Musical structures*:

A fifth of Beethoven by Walter Murphy, from the film, *Saturday Night Fever*. Courtesy of Thomas J. Valentino Inc., RFT Music Publishing Corp. (BMI)

Overture from *Elocution*. Performed by Killa Kela. Courtesy of Sony BMG Music Entertainment (UK) Ltd. Licensed by Sony BMG Commercial Markets UK.

Un granito de arena from *Cuban Legends: The Essential Ibrahim Ferrer* © 2006 Union Square Music Limited. Courtesy of Union Square Music Ltd, under exclusive license from Egrem.

Mind Swap © 2006 Ekstrak. Used with kind permission.

Montagues and Capulets © 2006 Ekstrak. Used with kind permission.

Quadrille performed by the Stars of St Petersburg, from the album *Balalaika: Russia's Most Beautiful Tunes.* ©℗ 1995 ARC Music Productions International Ltd.

Every effort has been made to trace and acknowledge copyright owners. If any right has been omitted, the publishers offer their apologies and will rectify this in subsequent editions following notification.